ALSO BY AMY LAURA DOMBRO:

THE ORDINARY IS EXTRAORDINARY:
How Children Under Three Learn
(with Leah Wallach)

◇

A FIRESIDE BOOK

published by

SIMON & SCHUSTER

■

New York

London

Toronto

Sydney

Tokyo

Singapore

Sharing the
CARING

How to Find the Right
Child Care and Make It Work
for You and Your Child

Amy Laura Dombro

and Patty Bryan

Simon & Schuster/Fireside

Simon & Schuster Building
Rockefeller Center
1230 Avenue of the Americas
New York, New York 10020

SIMON & SCHUSTER, FIRESIDE and colophon are
registered trademarks of Simon & Schuster Inc.

Designed by Liney Li
Manufactured in the United States of America

1   3   5   7   9   10   8   6   4   2
1   3   5   7   9   10   8   6   4   2 Pbk.

Library of Congress Cataloging-in-Publication Data

Dombro, Amy Laura
    Sharing the caring : how to find the right child care and make it work for
you and your child / Amy Laura Dombro and Patty Bryan.
        p.   cm.
    "A Fireside book."
    Includes index
    1. Child care—United States.   2. Child care services—United States.
I. Bryan, Patty. II. Title
HQ778.7.U6D66   1991   91-7705
649'.1—dc20   CIP
            ISBN 0-671-69077-9
                0-671-74094-6 Pbk.

ACKNOWLEDGMENTS

Many people have helped make this book possible.

I'd like to thank the parents of Alexander, Amelia, Angela, Becky, Carson, Dandara, Danielle, Danny, Dina, Gabrielle, Hannah, Irene, Katie, Lauren, Louisa, Luke, Matthew, Michael, Naomi, Nate, Nicholas, Raphael, Remy, Rico, Robbie, Sam, Sandy, and Steven as well as the caregivers and other early childhood professionals who talked with me about what it is like to share the care of young children. I have changed your names and at times a few details of your stories, but I hope you'll agree the essence of your experiences remains untouched.

To my colleagues who reviewed our manuscript—Barbara Abel, Susan Abrahams, Nancy Balaban, Amy Flynn, Laura Guarino, Judith Leipzig, and Vivian Newman—your thoughtful comments were very useful. I appreciate your help.

Joe, I'm grateful to you for introducing me to Patty.

And last, a special thanks to Mike for the hours spent surrounded by boxes going over our manuscript one last time and to Ed, for curing glitches and helping our computers talk with one another.

To Ed, my husband and my friend
—ALD

To all the kids in child care
—PB

Contents

Introduction

Each working day, several million mothers and fathers hand over their children to a third party—a caregiver. The Census Bureau estimates that 51 percent of *all* mothers with children under one year are now working mothers. Over 5 million preschool children are in child care in the United States. By 1995, almost 15 million children will have mothers in the labor force. Many of these children will be the focus of a parent-caregiver relationship.

In the past, children whose parents worked were usually cared for by members of their extended family—a grandmother or an aunt. Now that most nuclear families are "on their own" and a growing majority of women are working, parents must often share the care of their children with strangers. Both parents and caregivers want the best for the infants and toddlers they love and care for, and they therefore need to establish a mutual trust based on their shared caring for a child. Ideally, they form a partnership, building a bridge between home and child care, enabling children to feel safe and happy in both settings.

But parents and caregivers are often hindered in their bridge building by the complexity of their own relationship. Adults, often from extraordinarily different cultural, ethnic, social, and economic backgrounds, with various personal styles and philosophies of childrearing, are brought together caring for the same child. Both parents and caregivers are often insecure in their own roles and in their dealings with each other.

The idea of writing *Sharing the Caring* was born the day I realized that parents of children in the child-care center where I was working were as nervous and unsure about how to relate to me as I was uncertain how to work with them. I know one caregiver who never talked to a father because he was a doctor; she was convinced that he viewed her condescendingly as "only the caregiver." The father was so uncomfortable that he didn't know if he was even "allowed" to pick up his fourteen-month-old daughter when she began crying at the child-care center.

Soon I realized the basic problem: Busy with the child and their own lives, parents and caregivers don't have much time for *each other*. Communication is often negligible, and sometimes counter-productive. Young children evoke deep, raw feelings of love, ten-derness, jealousy, and competition in adults (it's almost impossible to live and work with a child under three and just go through the motions), and few parents or caregivers have the knowledge and skills they need to work harmoniously to support them.

Sharing the Caring addresses this problem. It is based on myriad interviews I have conducted with parents and caregivers from Ver-mont to Texas to California. As you read you can share their expe-riences and feelings; you will see that you are not alone. Every parent-caregiver relationship is unique because you and your care-giver and your child are unique, but there is much information and many skills that apply to all child-care situations.

Sharing the Caring is a book you can read by yourself, but I hope it's also a book you can read and discuss with your caregiver. Having something in print as a starting place may help you or your caregiver talk about an issue that otherwise might be considered off limits. Like any relationship, this one will have its ups and downs. There will be times you are in sync as well as times of strain and distance. The relationship between you and your caregiver, like any relationship, will take some effort. But it is well worth the work for the riches it can provide.

□   □   □

In Part I, we'll look at choosing child care. You want to find a setting in which you and your child will feel comfortable, but, like most parents, you will probably end up making some compromises in your final choice. The information in this part can help you decide which situations are workable for you and your family. If your child is already in child care, this part can help evaluate her experience and see what is working as well as areas you might need to improve.

In Part II we'll take a close look at the respective roles of parent and caregiver in your child's life, and the ideal relationship to establish. You will see that you each play a special role, and knowing who is who is key to building your relationship together. We'll also examine your feelings about sharing care and about each other and how your feelings can influence your relationship. Being aware of these feelings and how you deal with them is essential.

In Part III, we'll get down to the nitty gritty. We'll go into child-care settings and look at specific ways you and your child's caregiver can work together to help your child feel safe and secure—for example, by helping her begin the year, make connections between home and child care, and say hello and good-bye. We will also take a long look at ways to handle the inevitable differences that are sure to develop between you and the caregiver.

You and your child's caregiver are your own best assets when it comes to making child care work for your child. I hope you will find *Sharing the Caring* to be a valuable resource in your collaboration.

—A L D

PART ONE

Choosing Child Care

Having a child in child care is a decision you think about every day. It's so basic to everything. Being a good person means being sure your child is well taken care of. To get on with the rest of my life, to do my work I have to have confidence in the caregiver.

Choosing child care is not something you do automatically. As with many other aspects of parenting, you figure it out as you go along. You learn there are different types of child care, including in-home care, family child-care homes, and child-care centers. With legwork you find what is available in your area. You weigh such factors as your budget, the number of hours each day your child needs care, and the logistics of traveling between home, work, and child care. You visit child-care programs, interview caregivers, sort out your priorities, and finally choose a caregiver or program for your child.

A search for child care is individual. As you read

these chapters, take what is pertinent to your situation and make it yours.

Chapter 1

Starting with What You Know

Who your child is, what you want for her, and what your family's needs are—this is information you already have. Though its importance to your child-care decision may not be apparent to you, starting with a clear idea of what you know, but may not have thought about, will give you a head start in finding the care you want for your child.

You Know Your Child

Your child's age and personality can help determine what kind of child-care arrangement you choose. Your infant's unpredictable sleeping and eating schedule might sway you to opt for an at-home caregiver or for a willing grandparent. A toddler who stops to talk with everyone she meets may thrive in a setting with other children. A child who is easily overwhelmed by noise but likes company may do best with a neighbor who cares for one or two other children in her home.

You Know What You Want for Your Child

Most parents have one or two specific criteria that they especially want met when selecting a caregiver. A caregiver who speaks a second language is an increasingly common wish. Or you might feel strongly that you want a caregiver of a certain age or level of education. You might have to modify one or more criteria, or you might want to change your mind by the time you make your final decision, but know your own mind before you interview the first potential caregiver. A fairly common criterion was expressed by a woman in Vermont:

> *I wanted someone who had more experience and knew more than I did as a new mother. I find it comforting to have someone care for Dennis who knows, for example, about childhood diseases that I have never come up against. I also wanted someone who was clean, reliable and would give Dennis an interesting day.*

Other parents said:

> *I wanted someone kind and gentle. And someone who spoke Spanish.*

> *I want Jimmy to have an interesting day. I want him to feel free to walk around. A friend has her child with a woman who I'm sure is competent but she sometimes puts the kids in confined spaces such as playpens.*

> *If Sally can't be with us, we want her with someone who loves her.*

> *I wanted someone with no kids. I'd feel bad if she were leaving her child to take care of mine.*

You Know What Your Family Needs to Keep Running

Every family has an intricate set of arrangements that keep it functioning. You may not realize how intricate your own logistics are until you try to fit in child-care arrangements. Work schedules, travel time, and budgets will be affected by your child-care decision. It's worth keeping these things in mind as you make that decision.

You know the hours you need someone to take care of your child. If the program you are considering closes at 5:00 and you know there would be quite a few days when traffic would delay you until at least 5:30, don't sign up. If you need a caregiver to work from 6:00 to 3:00 and she can only work from 7:00 to 2:00, don't try to adjust your schedule to fit hers. Keep looking.

To see how location of child care might affect your plans for your child, ask yourself the following questions.

- Do you have any extra time to travel out of your way to drop off your child?
- Will the same person who picks your child up also drop her off?
- Are the travel arrangements so complicated you really require a caregiver to come to your home?
- Can an at-home caregiver provide her own transportation or will you have to?
- Will your child fall asleep on the way home and ruin bedtime?
- How does your child behave in a car, bus, or subway?

Last but not least, you know your family's finances. For some parents the cost of child care is of little concern, but for others tight budgetary control is required to pay for even the least expensive care. In some families, the second salary goes largely to child care. Some parents, because their company subsidizes child care, have the option of sending their children to programs that would ordinarily be beyond their means. Unfortunately, good child care is expensive, and its cost is a major factor for most parents. Only you can determine how much you can afford.

You Have Resources All Around You

While it's true that there is a nationwide shortage of child care for infants and toddlers, you only need to find care for your child. After you have carefully identified your own criteria, the next obvious job is to find out what's available in your community. There's only one rule of thumb in this regard: Use every resource.

Some sources are obvious. See if your workplace offers on-site child care or has an arrangement with a nearby program for employees' children. Ask the personnel department for information about local child-care programs. Look in the yellow pages to see if your community has a resource and referral service that lists child-care settings and providers in your area. Tell everyone you know that you are looking for child care. Speak with other parents, your pediatrician, your minister, your priest, or your rabbi. The neighbor standing behind you in line at the supermarket may know of a program or have a cousin looking for a job as an in-home caregiver. Check with the early childhood education department of your local college. Examine your local newspaper, flyers about community events, bulletin boards in your church, and the local bakery or copy store for ads about programs or caregivers.

Allow some time for these preliminary steps. Give yourself weeks, even months to think about your needs and learn the options in your community. If at all possible, avoid feeling rushed at any stage of the process. The decision may be difficult enough without the added pressure of time limitations. Only when you fully understand your needs and what's available out there is it time to make a fit between the two.

Chapter $\boxed{2}$

Which Kind
of Child Care?

If you live in a fairly large community, you will probably have located
the three traditional types of care.

- At-home care, in which a child is cared for by a private caregiver
  at home.
- Family child care, in which children spend their days in a small
  group in the child-care provider's home.
- Child-care centers, in which a staff of caregivers cares for groups
  of children.

There are also nontraditional arrangements that parents have devised on their own, such as "employing" grandparents, sharing a
caregiver with another family, or setting up a playpen at work. A
builder's son we know is watched at the worksite by a construction-
worker-turned-caregiver when his child-care home is closed.

The three traditional types of child care can differ in the amount
and quality of attention caregivers can give your child, as well as in
the accountability and dependability of the caregivers, the flexibility
of their hours, and the presence of other children. The strengths and
weaknesses of these options are *relative* to your individual wants and
needs, and also your child's. It's very possible that no single type of

child care is exactly what you want. Consider the following distinctions carefully.

Children Need Attention

Infants and toddlers need attention. Caregivers can only give a child the attention she needs if they have time to focus on each child in their care, and if their working conditions support that part of their job.

The amount of attention your child will receive is largely dependent on the number of children a single caregiver is responsible for (the child-caregiver ratio). If you have one child cared for by an at-home caregiver that ratio is 1:1. If your child is in a child-care program with fifty kids and there are five caregivers, the ratio is 10:1.

In a child-care center, be sure children are divided into groups. Ideally, no more than nine children should be cared for by three caregivers, for a 3:1 ratio. You are more likely to find a group of ten to twelve children with three caregivers. This 4:1 ratio isn't ideal, but it is commonly found. Any group larger than this becomes too confusing for children and caregivers alike.

With small enough groups, activities can still be planned around the specific interests of those particular children. When groups are too big, a caregiver spends most of her time managing daily routines rather than actively engaging the children.

Some states have regulations about child-caregiver ratio and group size. However, it's still up to you to evaluate those numbers, because your state's regulations may not be the best for your child, or they may not be enforced. Remember, the fewer children, the more responsive the caregiver can be.

For a family child-care provider, three to four infants and toddlers, with no more than two of them under the age of one, is an optimum group. More than two nonwalkers or new walkers limits the group's mobility for pleasure trips around the neighborhood and in emergencies.

Hiring a private caregiver for in-home care does assure a 1:1 child-caregiver ratio. A caregiver can immediately respond to your child's crying or the picture she drew. A caregiver can plan activities suited to your child's needs and interests, can arrange to be home from the park by your child's naptime, or can spend more time at the pet store simply because your child is captivated by the fish.

But before you automatically decide that one-to-one care is the only way your child will get the attention she needs, consider what each type of situation might mean from the caregiver's point of view. A caregiver at home with your infant or a caregiver alone in her own home with several children can feel isolated and become bored. Such a caregiver can easily burn out with the constant demands placed on her. A child with a private caregiver can end up watching a lot of television.

In a group setting, your child is not getting as much one-to-one care, in theory, but in practice caregivers working together can spell one another, share ideas, and keep one another company. In *qualitative* terms, they could actually have more to give to your child.

Ratio and group size are undeniably important, but your caregiver's working attitude and conditions are equally important to the amount of personal care your child will receive. Three happy, competent caregivers looking after ten children might be better than a single discontented caregiver in your home. Give all these factors serious consideration.

Children Need to be Safe

We have all heard stories about children being sexually abused and mistreated in child care. It's a rare occurrence, but it does happen. There are no guarantees. However, having other people around your child and her caregiver is a safeguard. The more public the setting, the less chance there is of abuse.

A center-based program is the most public type of child care. Parents and staff come and go throughout the day. Family child care is more public than private, and child care in your home is the most private. With private care, your child and her caregiver may not see another person until you return home.

If you choose to hire an in-home caregiver, you may want to consider building in some visibility, for example, by asking a neighbor to keep an eye on things when he or she sees your child and caregiver out around the neighborhood, or by arranging for your caregiver and child to spend time with other caregivers and children for part of the day. Regardless of the type of child-care arrangement, you should be able to drop by unannounced at any time, and you should do so occasionally.

Care You Can Count On

You depend on your child's caregiver to be there for you and your child. Her lateness or illness can turn your day into a disaster. Certainly a child-care center is the most secure arrangement. The director will deal with late staff members and assure adequate coverage. If a caregiver is ill or leaves, the program hires a substitute and carries on. This is not to say that caregivers are interchangeable. Things will be different for your child, especially if it is her special caregiver who is not there, but at least there will be someone on hand. Family child-care homes and private arrangements are left to the whim of the caregiver. If she is sick or decides to quit, you can be stuck.

The Chance to Play with Other Children

As children spend time together they begin to learn about being part of a community. Toddlers sit next to friends and share pieces of a bagel. They fight over the red shovel in the sandbox and become momentary enemies. With the caregiver's help, they find another shovel and dig holes together—friends again. They cooperate in carrying the card table from the closet to the middle of the room where it will be transformed into a tent, and they take turns hammering to fix a rocking chair. Even infants share this community experience. Watching the other children gives them much enjoyment and feeds their curious natures.

Child-care centers and family child-care homes guarantee children an opportunity to socialize. If you choose private child care, you will need to do some planning and you will require the cooperation of the caregiver to make and carry out arrangements for your child to spend time with peers.

Care That Fits Your Schedule

The different types of child care offer different degrees of flexibility. Private and family child-care schedules depend on what you and the caregiver agree to. A private or family child-care caregiver may be willing to work late occasionally, to come early, or to work on weekends—with sufficient compensation. A meeting that runs overtime and makes you late picking up your child or returning home doesn't usually create a crisis with private or family care. A child-care center, on the other hand, is open for set hours. You are expected to be on time at the end of the day—and you should be.

You know your particular criteria for child care. You have researched your community and know what's available. You have an idea of the pluses and the minuses of the three basic choices. Your decision now becomes *which* caregiver or child-care program you want for your child. You're ready for some field work.

Chapter 3

In-the-Field Investigation

Spending time in child-care settings and with caregivers is a prerequisite to making a decision about child care. Please do not make this decision on the basis of an advertisement or even a friend's recommendation. Your time in the field will be an invaluable investment in your child's well-being. Direct observation and assessment is the only way to get a sense of the person who will care for your child, the only way to get a sense of the place that will be her home away from home.

With caregivers who will be coming to your home, your job is mainly interviewing and checking of references, with some observation of the caregiver's interaction with your child. A child-care program will call heavily on both your interviewing *and* your observing skills. A child-care program is quite a complex environment. You will need to give it your full attention. But perhaps you aren't certain what to ask or what to look for. The following discussion will help you.

Who Will Care for Your Child?

The quality of care your child receives depends on having a caregiver who knows what she is doing. He or she—most commonly she—is responsible for planning your child's day. She keeps your child safe.

Her personality and style set the tone of the child-care environment. She will be your primary link to your child's child-care experience. Take time to find out as much as you can about any caregiver you want to employ.

□ *Interviewing*

You will get a better feel for the caregiver, and she for you, if life continues as usual during the visit. If a potential caregiver is coming to your house, stop if you find yourself reaching for the mop to go over the kitchen floor one more time. Your house doesn't have to be spotless, you don't have to wear your best clothes, your child doesn't have to be on her best behavior (as if you had control over this variable!).

When you visit a family child-care home or a child-care center, understand that the staff won't have freshly painted the place or rehearsed a show for you. Kids will be doing what they do—taking a nap, playing a game, or screaming at the top of their lungs. Caregivers will be doing what they do—leading some children in song, settling a disagreement, or changing a diaper. (In fact, in order not to interrupt what is going on, you will probably be asked to sit at the edge of the room and to be as unobtrusive as possible.)

During your interview, you want to find out not only about the caregiver but also about how she feels about children and working with you. You need to ask fact-finding questions, certainly, but you need to ask thought-provoking questions as well.

Facts you need to know range from how much experience a caregiver has to how much vacation time she wants. In center-based care, salaries, hours, vacations, and benefits such as insurance and sick days are spelled out. You and a private or family child-care provider need to be sure you have these points clearly arranged, preferably in a written agreement so everyone is clear about them, just as in any other business relationship. Giving your relationship this "professional" dimension does not undercut the intensely personal relationship the caregiver will have with your child, and perhaps with you. It is simply a way to avoid misunderstandings of the "you said

this, no I didn't" variety. We don't know how you feel about pre-
nuptial agreements, but precaregiving agreements make good sense.

In your interview you also want to learn whether you will be able
to work with this person to support your child. The goal is *not* to find
caregivers who will follow your every desire. Caregivers are people
with their own ideas and feelings, ones that might help you see
something about yourself or your child in a new light. The question
is not whether you will have disagreements—you will—but whether
you will be able to discuss them and work them out. This part of an
interview is very subjective.

During your time together, you will also be asked questions. Just
as you are looking for the right caregiver, caregivers look to see that
families and children fit with what they have to offer. The questions
you are asked can give you additional insight into the caregiver or
the program.

To assure that you get all your questions answered, we recommend you make a list before your interview of what you want to
know. Don't hesitate to have the list in hand at the interview.

Questions you might ask include:

Fact-finding questions:
- What, if any, credentials do you have?
- What is your training?
- What experience have you had caring for infants and toddlers?
- Who are your references?
- Is your program licensed?
- Do you smoke?
- What safety precautions do you take?
- What do you do all day with children?
- What are your hours?
- What are your fees?

Open-ended questions:
- Tell me a little about yourself.
- What do you like best about working with young children?

- What do you like the least? (Watch out for someone who loves all children and everything about them. You may want to press a little further. Children are individuals with distinct personalities. No one can like every child.)
- What would you do if my child had a temper tantrum in the middle of the sidewalk?
- How would you handle two children fighting for the same toy?
- What would you do if my child misbehaved?

Questions you may be asked include:

- What is your child's age?
- What hours do you need care?
- What do you want your child's child-care experience to be like?
- How do you see yourself being involved in the child-care program?
- Would you be willing to work on committees?
- Would you be willing to occasionally help out in the classroom? (Be sure the program's expectations of you match what you want to and can contribute.)

□ *Observing*

You mainly want to observe how a caregiver interacts with your child, or with the other children she is caring for. She may be nervous as you observe her initially, but you'll be able to see through that. She may not do certain tasks exactly as you do them but that is not what you are looking for. You're looking for the *presence* she has with children, the attitude she expresses, and reflections of experience she has had with children. Keep in mind the following as you observe:

Is she respectful?
- Does she give your child time to get to know her or does she swoop in and pick her up immediately?

- Does she listen to what a child says through actions as well as sounds and words?
- Does she talk with a child about the toy she holds up to show her, or is she too busy doing her thing to pay attention?
- Does she talk *with* children as opposed to talking *at* them?
- Does she encourage and applaud a toddler's attempt at a new skill, such as pouring juice or jumping, or does she shame the child for being clumsy?

Does she seem to enjoy children?
- Does she smile, laugh, and joke with them?
- Is she playful with the children?
- Does she get on the floor with them or does she stand aloof?

Do her interactions with children reflect her knowledge of developmental stages?
- Does she give an infant the opportunity to practice feeding herself by providing finger foods even if it means there will be some extra cleaning up to do?
- Does she encourage infants' language development by talking and reading with them even though they haven't yet said their first word?
- Does she give children legitimate, manageable choices, such as "Do you want to eat an apple or an orange for snack?" or does she overwhelm children with too many options, so that she will end up deciding anyway?
- Does she encourage rather than insist upon sharing by toddlers, who need to develop a stronger sense of self before they can be true sharers?

☐ *Checking References*

Combine the information you gather during your visit with a little research. Make a phone call or two. If you are hiring a provider to work in your home, call her references. If you are interviewing a family child-care provider or a caregiver in a program, talk to parents who have children currently enrolled. Listen to what they say *and* how they say it. Many people are uncomfortable giving a bad reference. Hesitation and a flat tone of voice may give you a feel for what is being said between the lines. Explain to the person that you are trying to find the best care possible for your child and would appreciate candor. Begin with these questions:

For private caregivers:
- How long did the caregiver work for you?
- What did you feel were her strengths and weaknesses?
- Would you hire her again?

For child-care and family caregivers:
- How long has your child been in the program?
- What things work best for you and your child?
- What are problem areas you see?
- How much turnover have you seen?

Where Will Your Child Spend Her Day?

A child-care setting should meet two major criteria. It should feel homelike, in order to help your child feel secure there, and it should assure your child's safety and health.

□ *Hominess*

Being "homey" away from home takes effort, since many child-care programs are housed in classrooms or church basements. Linoleum floors, fluorescent lights, and large open spaces work against the soft, cozy, warm feeling of a home. But being homey doesn't require an interior decorator. Some of the best programs take place in settings that are rather shabby looking, with blankets covering old chairs, remnant carpet pieces on the floor, and walls in need of a fresh coat of paint.

□   □   □

Think "house" when evaluating a child-care center for hominess. Can you find the following areas?

- A "living room" where children and caregivers spend most of their time together, talking, reading, playing, singing, and dancing. It might contain a sofa, shelves of toys, plants or fish, a rocking chair, and comfortable chairs where an adult and child can sit together reading, talking, or just being together.
- A "bedroom," a separate, quiet, well-ventilated space where children nap, each with her own crib or mat.
- A "kitchen" with table, sink, and counter. This is the place for eating snacks and lunch as well as for messy art projects.
- A bathroom.

When visiting a family child-care program, observe whether the caregiver's home is geared for children. If it looks like a four-page spread in *House Beautiful,* a house where keeping the carpet clean is more important than playing, your child's day will be filled with too many warnings of "don't touch," "no," and "be careful." However, a child-care provider doesn't want children to trash her house. She has to set some limits. It makes perfect sense that some rooms are closed off, and that she puts her vase of flowers on a shelf out of reach. She will enforce rules just as you do at home, such as *only* adults turn on the stereo and television. What you want to be sure of is that the provider's home is compatible with playing, exploring, scattered toys, and the occasional spilled juice that go hand in hand with active children. If it's not, look elsewhere.

Evaluate the hominess of any child-care setting not only by the division of the space into appropriate areas but also by the qualitative aspects of those areas. What's inside those rooms?

Is there a place where children can get away from the confusion and noise of group life? It takes energy to be involved in a group all day. Everyone needs some quiet time. Look for private getaways such as a house made of a cardboard box, a window seat, a loft space, or a tent made by throwing a cloth over a small table.

Does the space invite children's exploring?

- Are there different colors and textures?
- Is there room to crawl, run, and climb, as well as to sit quietly and read a book?
- Are toys within easy reach and labeled so children can find what they want rather than having to settle for whatever is at the top of a jumbled pile?

Does the space reflect the children's lives?

- Are family pictures hung at child level on the walls?
- Do toys and decorations reflect the cultural backgrounds of children's families?
- Is there space where each child can keep personal things?
- Are there books, bought or homemade, about meaningful events in children's lives, such as a visit to the doctor, getting dressed, and spilling milk?

Does the space help children feel competent?

- Are coat hooks low enough so toddlers can hang up and retrieve their own coats?
- Are sinks and toilets at child level so children can go to the toilet and wash their hands independently?
- Is there an overall sense of organization so children can find what they are looking for?

Do caregivers feel at home in the space? A setting that also takes caregivers into consideration nourishes the adults so they can be more available to children.

- Are there comfortable "adult" chairs?
- Do caregivers have places to hang their coats and other belongings?
- Is there a stove or hot plate for caregivers to make themselves a cup of coffee or tea?

Having real-life objects, the same ones that the children see their parents use at home, is another way of bringing "home" to child care, regardless of the type of child care. Expensive, slick toys are appealing to the eye but not necessary. Homemade toys, if safe and durable, can be wonderful. Kitchen equipment such as funnels, small colanders, and plastic measuring cups and spoons can provide hours of satisfying play. They can be the source of scientific discoveries such as floating and sinking, and invite the creation of endless "pretend" scenarios.

□ *Health and Safety*

You may assume that your child's safety and health are a given in a child-care setting, including your own home, but this is not always the case. Childproofing, emergency procedures, sanitary practices, and illness policies deserve your close attention.

Sooner or later your child will explore literally every corner of the place where she spends her day. Electrical outlets should be covered, sharp corners of tables padded, carpets secured so as not to trip a new walker. Harmful chemicals and other substances should be stored out of reach. This is especially important in a family child-care home where family members might naturally place detergent and bleach under the sink, or leave a pack of matches on the coffee table. If your child will be cared for in your own home, review your own childproofing procedures. Walk through your home to identify safety measures you should take, ranging from putting a guard across the stairs to storing the knife rack on a high shelf. It helps to get down on your knees or even lower to see your house from your child's eye level.

Ask about a program's emergency procedures. What would happen in case of a fire? Are there fire drills? How are accidents and injuries handled? What type of first-aid is available? Think through emergency procedures you want a home-based caregiver to follow. Ask a private caregiver what she would do in case of a fire. Ask if she has any first-aid training or would be willing to take a baby first-aid course with you. And in any setting make sure emergency numbers are posted near the phone.

You can try to prevent accidents and dispense Band-Aids for skinned knees, but you won't be able to prevent your child from getting sick occasionally. It's important that you and your child's prospective caregiver discuss what both of you will do when a cough, fever, or spots appear. A sick child can totally disrupt life for everyone concerned.

Ask in a child-care program what the policy is. You don't want to miss work for a runny nose, but a caregiver in a program can't be expected to care for a child who is truly sick. Most programs have guidelines to help you make decisions about when not to bring a child to child care, and to free the caregiver from being the "bad guy" who calls you away from work to pick up your child.

Discuss the question of illness when you interview a private caregiver. It may not be a concern of hers, unless perhaps she has never been exposed to measles or chicken pox. She may even be willing to take your child to the doctor. On the other hand, she may be uncomfortable caring for a sick child.

To protect your child's health, there are sanitary practices to look for when choosing any caregiver or program. Hand washing is number one. Caregivers should wash their hands after each diaper change and after wiping runny noses. Keeping the changing table sanitary is another essential. If disposable paper is used on the table, the paper must be changed with each diaper change. If not, the changing table should be wiped off with a diluted bleach solution after each change. Reminders to do both of these tasks should be posted so that everyone follows this routine.

What Will Your Child Do All Day?

Too often, child care is equated with school, caregivers with teachers, and infants and toddlers with students. It's natural that this happens, since school is the closest thing to group child care that many adults know. But when we stop to look carefully at infants and toddlers, we see that child care is or should be very different from our idea of school. Of course the children learn, as in school, but they learn mainly through interacting with their caregivers and with the other children. Of course caregivers teach, but they teach mainly as they interact with the children, change their diapers, listen for car horns on walks, and clean up after snacks.

Therefore, curriculum for infants and toddlers should be based primarily on everyday activities, with lots of room for special activities such as making play dough and painting. But none of these activities is any more valuable than a child helping prepare snacks, repair a torn page in a book, or carry home a bag of pears from the fruit market.

Participating in everyday routines, dressing, eating, diapering, taking a walk, preparing snacks, helps your child feel connected to you since these everyday chores are the same kinds of things your child does at home with you. At home and in child care, daily routines are wonderful learning opportunities. Their repetition, which makes daily routines so boring for us, gives your child the opportunity to understand what is happening, to feel competent and capable. By participating in the real work of her child-care family, sliding a chair to the snack table, buttering toast for breakfast, or putting the paper towels and cups away under the sink, your child comes to feel that she belongs. She feels valued and proud. She feels at home in her "other" setting.

Making a "snack" is one of many everyday activities in which Alice, a caregiver, purposefully includes children. A behind-the-scenes glimpse of the children and Alice as they make French toast will demonstrate how a "daily activities" curriculum works.

□   □   □

Alice invites children over to the table to join her to make French toast for a snack. Four two-year-olds—Gary, Lyle, Becky, and Henry—take her up on her offer.

"The first thing we have to do is stir these eggs together." While Alice holds the bowl, Gary heartily stirs some of the eggs up over the edge of the bowl. As he is about to taste the overflow, Alice explains raw eggs are not good to eat and wipes his finger clean. Next to him, Lyle and Becky begin poking each other. Lyle ups the ante by spitting. Alice reminds the children that she does not want children to spit at each other. "Use your words," she says as she reaches for the loaf of bread the two have begun pulling apart. "We'll need this bread later," she explains. "Can you two try to wait a minute . . . I know it is hard to wait . . . but then you can have a turn stirring.

"It's time to pass the bowl to Lyle so he can stir," Alice says to Gary, who fails to respond. She tries another approach: "OK, now, let's count to five and then you can pass the bowl." Gary continues stirring. "Do you want to try counting to five again? Lyle and the other children need a turn to stir. You have to pass the bowl now, Gary. I'm sorry if it makes you angry."

Across the table Henry dumps the can of cinnamon. "Do you want to help me wipe up the spilled cinnamon?" Alice asks. She hands Henry a sponge.

Lyle, who has finally gotten a turn to stir, dabs a finger in the cinnamon. His eyebrows crinkle as he tastes it.

"That's cinnamon," explains Alice. "See, its name is right here on the can. Do you like the way it tastes?"

Lyle nods yes.

"Yuck," says Becky, who also takes a taste. "Me no like cinmon."

"I like the taste of cinnamon," shares Alice. "Would you like to put a sprinkle of some cinnamon into the French toast batter?" she asks Henry. He does.

Alice takes a turn giving a stir and then asks for volunteers to dip the bread into the egg and milk mixture. She gives each child a piece of bread and as Henry and Lyle eat their bread, the others dip and place the wet bread on a plate. Alice places the bread in the frying pan, located up out of children's reach on the counter, takes a deep breath and invites the children to sing "Twinkle, Twinkle Little Star," a group favorite, while they wait for the French toast to cook.

Five rounds of the song later, Alice passes around a platter offering children the chance to choose bite-sized pieces of the French toast they helped make.

This fifteen-minute daily activity contained many lessons for the children. The children's language skills were called upon, health and safety issues were presented, numbers were practiced, songs were sung from memory, limits were set, and cooperation was encouraged.

When you are trying to evaluate the curriculum a child-care program or an individual caregiver will offer your child, consider the following factors.

Do the caregivers take advantage of everyday activities to help children feel competent and secure?

- Do the caregivers let children participate as much as they are able to in daily routines, such as changing diapers, making snacks, and getting dressed?
- Do the caregivers talk with the children about what they are doing?
- Do they invite children to respond and listen to what they have to say?

Do caregivers take the individual needs of children into account?

- Do daily routines of eating, sleeping, and using the toilet take into account children's individual likes and dislikes and schedules?
- Are children allowed to pursue their interests, or are they all forced to sit around a table together to do adult-initiated activities such as gluing or painting?

Do caregivers help children learn to think and solve problems?

- Is a caregiver able to step back and let a child try to come up with a solution to a problem, such as how to build a road with blocks, make a mobile move, or fit a piece in a puzzle, or does she always jump in with a quick-fix solution? Knowing when to step back is as important a skill for caregivers as knowing when and how to intervene.
- Does a caregiver show she values thought by acknowledging children's ideas ("Pulling over that box to stand on so you could reach is a good idea") and by sharing her own thought processes ("I wonder if this oil will stop the squeak in our door? Let's try it and see").
- Are there times the caregiver directly and respectfully teaches children how to do something? ("First, sit down. Next, put one leg at a time through your pants. Then stand and pull your pants up. You did it!")

Who's the Boss?

In addition to paying attention to how your child will be treated in a child-care arrangement, you must also reflect upon how you will be regarded. Your child needs you to be part of her child care on two levels. She needs you to be there physically at times, to help her feel at home and to keep track of what is happening, and your child needs you, the person who knows her best of all, to be the ultimate authority where she is concerned. Caregivers should make it clear that you are a welcome part of her child-care experience.

The child-care program must be open to you whenever you want to come. You shouldn't have to have an appointment to be with your child. You shouldn't be viewed as an interruption or disruption, but programs do exist in which this is the case. We know a program in which caregivers greet children and parents at the front door. Not allowed inside, the parents say good-bye as the caregiver takes away the children. The children are changed into standard outfits that they wear all day until they are changed and carried to the front door to meet their parents. The underlying message about family is frightening. Don't put your child in such a program.

You also have to feel that caregivers will be willing to address your questions and concerns and will be willing to listen to you. You want to have a say in factors that affect your child's life when you are not there, such as what food is served, whether your child should go out when it's cold, or whether cloth or paper diapers are used. You must feel that your wishes for your child are respected. This is *your* child you are talking about. The final word belongs to you.

Chapter 4

Making a Decision

You have determined what you want for your child and what you need to keep your family running. You've observed child-care programs and spoken with caregivers. And you've probably realized that no one place or person meets all your criteria. So how do you make the final decision?

Making the final decision means weighing pros and cons and deciding what is *most* vital to you. Choosing child care almost always involves making compromises. Only you can decide what is workable for your child and your family.

Many families combine types of care. These arrangements work well *if* there is a regular pattern that children can depend on, and *if* there aren't an overwhelming number of changes for the child. One child may spend mornings at a child-care center and afternoons at home with a private caregiver. Another child may spend three days a week in family child care and two days at home with grandparents.

These mix-and-match solutions are fine, but try to avoid one that has two settings on Monday, two *different* settings on Tuesday, and so on. Don't laugh. Parents have tried these schedules out of desperation, but that's the only time they should be used: Desperation.

One parent felt that a child-care center wasn't as clean as she would have liked it to be. After thinking about how hard it was for her to keep her own house clean, with only one child, after calculating how much fees would have to be raised to pay someone to clean the center, and after seeing how the caregivers always had room on their laps for another child, she decided to enroll her child.

Sarah and Leslie's parents had a different idea of "eating right" than the family child-care provider up the road, who thought the girls should eat only foods that were 100 percent natural. The convenience of location and the warmth of the caregiver made it less important that she never gave the girls cookies or candy, which they sometimes ate at home.

Tim's parents were upset that his child-care provider watched her soap opera every afternoon. Tim, whom they describe as a "videophile," would watch with her. But when they thought about the cooking, walks, painting, and reading Tim did during the rest of the day with the caregiver, his parents decided an hour of television was acceptable.

As you make your choice don't forget your intuition, a resource you rely on in many parts of your life. Trust your gut. Your feelings are one of your most important resources as a parent . . . at home and at child care. A father we talked with said he knew from the beginning that his daughter's child-care center would be fine. He said it felt like finding their apartment in New York City. He walked in and knew that was it. A mother says that the first time Winnie, a caregiver, picked up her son, she knew she would hire her.

But finding child care is just the beginning. Your child needs you to continue the process of observing and talking with caregivers, needs you and the caregiver to keep in tune with how each of you feels about what's happening. It's not only the situation, but what you give to it, that is important for you and your child. No matter how good the child care, your child needs you to make it better. That's what the rest of this book is about.

Roles and Relationships: Parents and Caregivers

It took us a while to develop a parent-caregiver relationship. First I had to find out who I was as a parent. My son's caregiver had to figure out who she was as the teacher in charge of a classroom. Then we could begin working together.

Finding a caregiver or a child-care program for your child doesn't mean your work is over. In fact, it has hardly begun. You are now faced with the fact that you are sharing the care of your child with someone else. Is that possible?

The mother's statement quoted above gets straight to the heart of the question. In order to share the care of your child, you and your caregiver have to have a thorough understanding of your unique roles in your child's life. You also need to have an understanding of the relationship that you build to support those roles. In this section, the roles of parents and caregivers will be clearly defined. We will give you insight into building a strong parent-caregiver relationship so you will be ready to deal constructively with the host of situations and problems that may crop up.

Chapter 5

Who Is Who

It is common for parents and caregivers to blur or confuse their roles, and the confusion of roles on either part can only be a hindrance to your child and her child-care experience. You are the most important person in your child's life. No one can take your place. Don't let the fact that you and the caregiver do many of the same caregiving activities (dressing, feeding, changing, playing with, and so forth) make you lose sight of who is who. You and your child's caregiver have extremely different roles in your child's life. Your child certainly knows the difference. You and your child's caregiver should know this, too.

How You Are Different

The roles of parent and caregiver offer your child different amounts of investment, different degrees of trust, different perspectives, and different personal histories. Being clear about these factors that set you and your caregiver apart will make it much easier for you to work together.

□ *The Connection You Make*
Your relationship with your baby is forever. It will continue over the years and across the miles. Although you may be with your child for fewer of her waking hours Monday through Friday than her care-

giver is, your status as mother or father is part of the essence of who she is and who you are. It is a mutual relationship you are both greatly invested in.

A caregiver's connection with your child is temporary. A caregiver working in a child-care center says, "I feel a kid knows their parent will always be there. It's not the same with me."

But even though your caregiver's relationship with your child is fleeting compared to your relationship, the connection they do establish is meaningful and can have a strong and lasting influence on your child. Jenny, an eleven-year-old, went back to visit her old child-care center. The real purpose of her visit to the center was to invite Francis, who had been her special caregiver and was now the director, to her sixth-grade graduation. Jenny had been asked to speak during the ceremony and one of the things she planned to talk about was her memories from the child-care center. Obviously, the relationship that Francis and Jenny developed was very important to Jenny.

☐ *The Trust You Provide*

Your child trusts you more deeply than she trusts her favorite caregiver, and that's a major difference in your roles. She knows you will be there for her no matter what she does or how she feels. She trusts you to keep things from getting out of hand as she explores her feelings to their depths. She is her happiest, silliest, saddest, and most defiant with you. Her biggest and best hugs as well as her loudest "no's" are reserved for you. Many parents have or will experience a situation similar to the following.

The mother of a seven-month-old infant chances leaving the office a few minutes early so she can get to the child-care center and be with her infant, whom she has been missing all day. As she stands in the doorway, he spots her from where he is sitting on a caregiver's lap listening as she reads a story to a small group of toddlers. He breaks into tears.

"But he was fine all day," the caregiver reports as she hands this crying baby over to his mother.

□   □   □

This unexpected response is actually a declaration of this child's trust in his mother. The minute his mother walks into the room, he is safe in a way he hasn't been safe all day. Because he trusts that his mother will be there no matter what he does, he can relax and express what he is feeling. Perhaps he couldn't fall asleep at naptime and is tired. Perhaps he has been working hard to hold himself together; it can be hard work spending all day in the bustle of a group setting. He is so full of feelings that they overwhelm him and break forth.

By being there for your child—to help when she gets stuck in her first attempts to roll over, to try to figure out what she wants as she points to a crowded counter, to listen to her story about making pancakes with Grandma—your caregiver develops a trusting relationship with your child, too. She's building on what you have started and confirming your message to your child that she can count on other people. But your child's trust in her caregiver is not absolute. Here's a story that illustrates this fact.

A caregiver once volunteered to help out in a children's house on a kibbutz. The children lived with women from the community who were called *metapeluts.* Every day parents would come to visit on this particular kibbutz. The visitor observed that children would go to their metapeluts to tie their shoes or for a hug if they tripped and fell during their parents' visit. She wondered if this meant the connection between parent and child was being weakened by the involvement of another significant caregiving adult in the family's life. Then came the night of the air raid. As everyone ran for shelter, children reached out for the ultimate safety of their parents' arms. Children know who is who in their lives.

Nor is your child's trust automatic. A new skill your child has acquired and performs regularly at home—drinking from a cup, walking, using the potty—may disappear for a while in front of your caregiver.

□   □   □

Emily had taken her first steps at home over the weekend. Throughout the next week the caregivers kept their eyes on her but all she did was crawl around as usual. It wasn't until Thursday, when Emily's mother came to eat lunch with her, that Emily took her first step at child care. Starting from the security of her mother's lap, she stood up and took fifteen steps before plopping down on her bottom and joining everyone in their applause. It was another week before she would walk around the child-care center on her own.

□ *Your Point of View*

In your parental role, your view of your child is subjective. Your passions run deep. You feel a crazy kind of love for your baby—for the crinkle in her pudgy knee, her toothless grin, the wisp of hair that curls against her neck. This kind of love lets your child know how special she is. Where your child is concerned, your feelings are strong. Your devotion to her makes you her best advocate.

This deep connection between parent and child makes it difficult, if not impossible, to step back and be impartial, even in the case of a mother who is a child psychologist. She became very upset when her toddler son began saying "No." Even though she knew that toddlers say "No" to declare their independence and define who they are, it was different when *her* child was saying "No." Her feelings overwhelmed her reasoning. She worried something was wrong.

Your child's caregiver's role allows her to be more objective. Her relative emotional detachment allows her to step back from a situation. Temper tantrums are no fun for anyone but they are a little easier on her. Watching your child go through some rough stages or learn a new skill like drinking from a cup may be very frustrating for you but it's all in a day's work for a caregiver.

A caregiver in New York City shares a convincing story regarding the objectivity her role allowed:

*I am an important part of a child's life, but the children and
I are not as invested in each other as children are with their*

parents. *A temper tantrum, for example, is not the same with me as with a child's parent. I can more easily stand back and not get lost in my feelings as a parent might do.*

Yesterday, Rebecca sat down on the sidewalk on the corner of Broadway and 110th Street because she wanted me to carry her. I couldn't. We had just walked to the fruit market and I was carrying several bags of apples we were going to make into applesauce for a snack.

"Carry," she said, pouting, sitting there on the sidewalk.

People walked by looking at her and then looked at me as if I was some kind of ogre.

"My arms are filled with these apples," I explained. I even offered her the opportunity to help me carry some.

"Carry," she said again, this time more insistently. Then she started crying. She lay down and began kicking at me. I knelt beside her trying not to notice the stares of passersby.

In two or three minutes she began calming down. I explained about the apples. She looked at me. I rubbed her back and said, "Let's go so we can get back to the center and make applesauce."

She stood up with her eyes on the sidewalk. Was she a bit embarrassed? I wondered. She reached up to hold my hand.

Rebecca isn't my child. Sure I felt annoyed at her and a little embarrassed by people looking at us—but nothing like if she had been my daughter. I speak from experience. My daughter, who is now fifteen, used to spend lots of time sitting and lying on the sidewalk. It drove me crazy.

□ *What You Know*

Your roles are also distinguished by your different personal histories. You and your child's caregiver come together with different background information. Yours is the history of you and your own child. Hers is a collective history, gathered from working with many unrelated children. Your information is intimate and unique; hers is an overview of children, broad and general. You know how your child likes to be held, you usually know the difference between her hungry and angry cries, you know her favorite songs and toys. A caregiver knows patterns of child development, she has the skills needed to organize and implement daily routines with one or more children, and she has a collection of time-tested ideas of interesting and fun activities for your child.

Your knowledge can help your child's caregiver tune in to the special qualities of your child. The caregiver's knowledge can broaden your vision, helping you see your child on a spectrum of development. Your different stores of information will give both of you a more complete picture of your child. You know that your child likes apples better than oranges, she falls asleep on her stomach, and she's not afraid of dogs. Your caregiver knows that a one-year-old drawing on walls indicates that the child is simply moving out into "space," not that she is becoming a graffiti artist, she knows that children from sixteen to eighteen months old can't sit still a long time, and she knows that eventually *every* child, even yours, is toilet trained.

What You Have in Common

Besides sharing many caregiving activities, you and your caregiver share some basic human traits. It may seem unnecessary to spell out that in your role as parent *or* caregiver, you will need self-respect, you will learn and grow, you will not be and don't need to be perfect, and you will need help at times. But we often overlook the obvious.

□ *The Need for Self-respect*

In your role as a parent or a caregiver, you need to feel good about your work. Our society makes this very difficult. For caregivers, choosing to work with infants and toddlers is choosing a profession that ranks almost at the bottom of the totem pole. Yet to do their job, which can appear to be just playing with children and cleaning up spilled juice, caregivers have to have more knowledge and sensitivity than people working with any other age group.

Our society's views make it difficult for parents too. A dad has to sneak out of his office on the days he picks his daughter up at her family child-care home. His fellow workers might consider his leaving early to be "goofing off," even if he took unfinished work home. A mother of an infant says, "When people ask me what I do and I say I'm a mother, they don't pay much attention. But if I talk about my work at the office, they are really interested. It's hard because being a mother to me is the most important thing I do and no one wants to hear about it."

Given these circumstances, how *do* you maintain respect for yourself, how do you fulfill this part of your role as a parent or caregiver? Acknowledging how much you accomplish for your child, and not taking your actions for granted, can be a start in helping you and your caregiver give yourselves the respect you deserve. Consider the constant decision making you do every day, the skill it takes to communicate with a young child, and your ability to design an environment that encourages your child's curiosity and helps her feel competent. Those skills would be highly regarded in any profession.

A caregiver who was earning her M.S. in early childhood development explained how she maintained her dignity and defended her chosen profession:

> *Sometimes my friends kid me about going to graduate school to take care of babies. Sometimes I myself can't believe that I'm getting a master's degree to spend my days changing diapers. When someone says something about it, I reply, "Yes, but I give quality diaper changes."*

□ *Room to Grow*

Another similarity in your roles is that both parent and caregiver will be learning and growing as they care for a child. Living or working with infants and toddlers makes adults aware of how much they have to learn, are learning, and, as time passes, have learned.

Being aware of your own development can help you tune in to the excitement and frustration that is a necessary part of all learning, for you and your child alike. You know that learning something new takes time, with steps forward, and often steps backward. This understanding can help you be supportive rather than frustrated or worried when you see your child struggling with a new skill. Knowing how good it feels to realize you've "gotten it" will let you share your child's pleasure at her new accomplishments.

But sometimes it takes stepping out of your daily routine to recognize what you have learned. A couple went to a reunion of their Lamaze class. The father was able to see how far he had come in four months as a parent.

> *I've learned how to diaper a baby. And I don't panic when Yvonne cries, like I thought I would. I walk around with her. One night we even ended up riding around the neighborhood in the car until she quieted down. Four months ago everything was a big question mark . . . what would it be like to have a baby? . . . could we manage? I think we can.*

At a weekend training workshop, a caregiver shared with colleagues some activities that she had created during the past year. Her ideas were met with great enthusiasm and an eagerness to try them. The feedback from her colleagues made the caregiver realize she had developed something worthwhile for the child-care community at large.

A mother of an infant learned something about herself through observing the caregivers in her son's child-care center:

> *When Jake was an infant he wasn't sleeping, and I was struggling and exhausted. I felt thrown on my own resources with this new baby, and I wanted help. At the child-care center I saw people more experienced than me who seemed warm, loving, and positive.*
>
> *My pattern had always been that if I didn't like something, I got mad. But that doesn't work. I knew positive reinforcement worked better. I needed a new script. I was struggling with the question, "How do you change someone's behavior?" It was a*

question relevant to my teaching of college students, to my marriage, and to being a mother.

One day I saw Cynthia, the director of the center, seating toddlers for snack. "Do you want a fork or a spoon?" she asked them. She gave the one child who didn't answer a spoon.

He threw it across the floor and screamed, "Fork!"

I was aware there was another way of handling the situation besides getting mad, but I wasn't sure what it was. I had the chance to sit back and watch. I saw that Cynthia, was completely unaffected emotionally by this child's spoon throwing. It was no skin off her nose.

She didn't get mad and she didn't have to stifle her anger. She picked up the spoon and said to the toddler, "I'm glad you told me. That's why I asked. But if you don't want the spoon, it's better to hand it to me."

I had the revelation that you can let things go. I walked away with that. I digested this as a new way of responding. It filled the hole where I was getting mad. I took to hanging out at the center as much as I could so I could soak up what it feels like to see people teach positively.

It is important to your child that you and her caregiver continue to grow and learn in your respective roles. She benefits by being around questioning and growing adults. It's a tremendous advantage for her to be with adults who are open and reflective. There's a kind of energy that comes with growing that she can hook on to. Seeing you try new things, hearing you ask questions says to her that these things are important. If you are doing these things she will want to do them too.

□ *No Need for Perfection*

Parents and caregivers constantly forget that being perfect is godlike, not humanlike. They think that fulfilling their roles includes reaching a state of perfection. But there are flaws inherent in striving to be the perfect parent or caregiver. This striving creates unrealistic goals and pressures for you and your caregiver, it assumes that there is always a right and a wrong way to care for a child, and it erroneously equates doing the *perfect* thing with doing the *best* thing for your child.

In striving to be perfect parents, people make unrealistic demands on themselves. Trying to be perfect, many working parents find themselves operating in the "make-up" or "deficit" mode as they feel pressure to make up for lost time with their children. There is no question that having a child in child care means losing some time with her. But it's important not to let these feelings take over.

Parents unrealistically try to make every minute that they spend with their child perfect. When you have only two hours after work to spend with your child, you want things to be just right. But trying to spend these two hours perfectly only increases tension. It's helpful to remember that every day, as you help your child dress, drive to child care, bathe, prepare dinner, your relationship grows and your child learns—about herself, about her world, and about relationships. You don't have to be perfect for that to happen.

Parents and caregivers are constantly faced with new questions and challenges ranging from the theoretical to the mundane. There is *no* perfect answer to any of these questions. What does being a good parent mean? How can I help my child feel good about herself? How do I share my values? How do I set limits? How do I toilet train her? For caregivers questions might include How can my program support children's learning? How can I help Joany feel more at home? Why doesn't naptime seem to be working this year? Should we have goldfish or hamsters for a class pet? How can I keep the Legos from always getting dumped over?

It's a relief for parents and caregivers to see themselves struggling with the same issues. Sandy forced her son into his car seat one day. He wasn't cooperating and she got mad. She said that at the height of her anger she hated him and herself. She cried when she related the incident to her husband. The next day she asked her caregiver, Mary Ann, what she should do when she has to "muscle" her child. Mary

Ann's answer clearly showed how she struggles with the same issue: "I do it as fast as I can and I look the other way."

The idea that your being perfect all the time is the best for a child is perhaps where parents and caregivers go most astray. The fact is your child doesn't need *either* of you to be perfect. It's not in her best interest. She needs you to be human, needs to see you struggle, needs to see your moments of imperfection as well as the moments when you have it all together.

You will never be a perfect parent. There is no such thing as a perfect caregiver either. You both make hundreds of decisions a day. Sometimes you make mistakes. But over time you will gain confidence and come to know that everything will be OK even if it turns out—and it certainly will at some time or another—that you made a mistake. There will be plenty of opportunities for you to be right and wrong. Accepting that you don't have to be perfect can remove a lot of pressure.

□ *The Need for Support*

Along with not having to be perfect, neither of you has to "go it alone" in your respective roles. The reality is that no one can give, give, give without being given to. Children are not the only people who need to be taken care of and supported. It's fair to get help. And that's part of your role—incorporating support for yourself.

But finding support for yourself requires some planning and can feel like just another chore to fit into your already crowded days. However, the effort you spend will be worth it. Think about what you need in order to feel nurtured. Think about who in your life can be there for you—your partner, your own parents, friends, colleagues?

Perhaps what you or your caregiver needs is similar to the needs of these mothers:

Sometimes I wish I could trade places with my son Jamie. We worry about him. We talk about him. When we have to say good-bye in the morning, a caregiver is there to give him a hug.

When I close the door of that child-care center, I have to walk to the subway and go to work by myself. There is no one to give me a hug.

My boss was upset when I missed work two days in a row because my son was sick. She feigned sympathy and said she had been a working mother too. But it was very clear that all she really was concerned about was that I hadn't been there to make phone calls and file papers. It made me furious. It would have made all the difference if instead of her berating me, we could have worked together to plan how I could make up the time missed.

A caregiver was helping a family deal with separation. The child was crying all the time and the mother was calling the caregiver constantly. Both parent and child were driving the caregiver crazy. Discussing the situation with the director of her program allowed the caregiver to vent her frustrations and get some advice. In turn, she was able to "be there" for the child and parent.

The single father of a two-year-old was beside himself. It seemed as if his child had turned into a demon overnight. She was constantly testing and nothing he did made things any better. Spending an evening sharing stories with friends, also parents of a two-year-old, gave him the relief of knowing that his daughter was not indeed turning into a demon and that he was not alone in feeling over-whelmed by such new behavior. Talking to other parents allowed him to take a breath and feel more confident that he and his daughter would make it to her third birthday.

Maybe you need just a little relief in your schedule. Louise, a care-giver, made an arrangement with her teenaged son to relieve her from kitchen duty on the day she works late. He prepares dinner on that day and she makes pancakes, his favorite breakfast, on Saturday mornings.

Tom, a single father, and his two toddlers spend Sunday afternoons with his parents. The children enjoy being with "Ma" and "Pa-pa," Ma and Pa-pa enjoy their grandchildren, and Tom gets a break from being on duty, as well as a visit with his parents and a home-cooked meal.

Both parents and caregivers need child-free time—time to pursue their own interests or just to relax. Karen, a single mother, and her sister trade off taking care of their children every other Saturday. Annie and Richard, parents of Simone, have arranged for the teen-aged girl who lives down the street to come and stay with Simone every Friday night so they can go out for dinner or a movie and have some time to talk and be together. Ed, another single father, makes time to referee at a community basketball game once a week. How you spend your child-free time is of course up to you. The important thing is that you do find the time and enjoy it.

Chapter 6

Between Parent and Caregiver

Your relationship with the caregiver will be the foundation for your child's child-care experience. Your child needs you to have a dynamic, working relationship that will serve as a link between home and child care, even if she is cared for in your own home. She needs her parents and caregivers to be colleagues acting in her best interest.

Like any worthwhile relationship, yours with your caregiver will take some effort, including acknowledging your feelings about sharing care, showing respect for each other, communicating with each other, and, mundane as it may sound, *not being late*. Whatever it takes for you and your caregiver to have a strong relationship, it's well worth it for your child.

How You Feel About Sharing Care

Sharing the care of your child means introducing someone else into her life and eventually leaving her with that person. If a child's parents have complicated feelings about *their* sharing her care, it is no surprise that you and her caregiver will have these feelings, too. You will each have different emotions over the course of your relationship. They are to be expected. They are healthy but sometimes painful feelings based in the deep attachment you each feel for your child—an attachment she needs. Recognizing these feelings for what they are will prevent their being misplaced or misunderstood, coloring your perceptions about how your child is doing, or hindering your relationship.

We are going to look at some feelings experienced by many parents and caregivers: Feelings of "letting go," feelings of doubt and inadequacy, jealousy, guilt, and resentment. Knowing that these feelings—and others—go hand in hand with sharing care means you don't have to worry that something is wrong when you experience them. You don't have to feel embarrassed, either. Rather than trying to cover them up—a very common response—you can examine where they're coming from. You may find it helpful to talk about them with your mate or another parent, and in some cases with your caregiver. The point is not to change your feelings; you feel what you feel. But knowing you are not alone and talking about them can give you some relief and help you keep them in perspective. Let's look at these common feelings and see how they get in the way of sharing the care of your child.

☐ *Feelings of "Letting Go"*

For many parents who place their children with caregivers, feelings about "letting go" are among the first emotions they have to deal with. These feelings can manifest themselves in as many ways as there are parents. They can be overwhelming at the time. Although they usually don't have a long-lasting effect on your relationship, it's worth sharing a few parents' reactions when they were faced with "letting go."

One mother worried for a whole month about the first day she would leave her child with someone else. Her worry was grounded in her concern that someone else would be watching her child grow up. When the day finally came, she cried her eyes out. She said handing over her child to one of the caregivers was like losing her best friend, or like someone had died. She felt she would never see her child again. She called five times from work that day to check on

her child. By the afternoon, after a highly charged emotional out-
burst in the morning, she was able to at least focus on her work. She
knew she would be OK.

Another mother described her visceral reaction to the initial place-
ment of her child in child care and her surprise at that reaction: "I
cringed. I felt it in my gut. It is a wrenching feeling. And this was after
spending two months at home with him before I went back to work.
I could still function, but barely. I'm usually more businesslike, more
'let's get on with it.'"

A third mother's feelings about turning over the daily care of her
child led her to believe that having a caregiver wouldn't work out.
There wasn't anything wrong with the caregiver. The mother just
didn't know if she could hand over her very young child to someone
else. After the caregiver had been there only a few days, the mother
turned over the bathing of her son. Then she heard her child crying
in the tub. She said it broke her heart to stay out of the bathroom. It
broke her heart to begin letting go.

□ *Feelings of Doubt and Inadequacy*

We all tend to cover our feelings of doubt and inadequacy. No one
wants to feel like a bumbler. Like your child, you, too, are in an
exciting, challenging, but vulnerable stage of your life. Placing your
child in child care only heightens this uneasiness. Faced with a caregiver who can get a *group* of children ready for a walk to the park
while you find yourself mounting a major effort to get *one* child out
the door in the morning, your confidence as a parent can start to
erode. As you hand over your child to her caregiver you may find
yourself handing over your sense of authority as well as your feeling
of competence. If you do so, you may inadvertently turn your caregiver into an intimidating expert.

Faced with parents who have questions at every turn and having
the answers for *some* of them, it is easy for caregivers to "know it all."
Having "raised" more children than most parents, some caregivers

find it easy to presume more competence. Spending more time with a child than some parents, caregivers find it seductively easy to assume parental privileges. And since society lacks respect for their work, this is a way to feel important. But taking on this role of expert could be a caregiver's way of hiding her own doubts about her competence. You may have tried this strategy yourself at one time or another.

Two caregivers explain how they have been tempted to become "the expert":

> *It is difficult for me not to assume the role of expert. It's seductive when parents look to you for answers. The less information you have, the easier it is to assume the role of expert. When I first began working as a caregiver it was difficult for me to share questions—to admit I didn't know.*

> *At first I saw myself as an expert. I thought that's what parents wanted me to be. I read and read. I'd stay up late nights trying to memorize what Penelope Leach and Berry Brazelton have to say.*

But most experienced caregivers see the trap of "expertness," and are on the alert. They realize they have information and skills that parents can use, but they also realize they can impart this information in a way that will make parents feel *more* rather than less competent. Caregivers who give too many answers deprive parents of the opportunity to learn and make decisions and grow in their role.

> *It took me time to figure out that giving answers is not my place. I'm twenty-six. I'm not a parent. I think it's OK to say "I don't know." What I can do is look at a situation with a parent—I can listen and observe, I can ask questions and try to help solve the problem.*

> *I'm getting better in my third year—now I can open up meetings to the parents rather than give all my answers.*

I've had the experience of being cast in the role of a savior, the
expert. It is easy to be seduced and soothe the parent. But when
I'm at my best, I reflect back to parents what they say. My goal
is to empower parents—not just give information.

☐ *Feelings of Jealousy*

Jealousy, another common feeling that stems from strong attach-
ments to children, often originates when parents and caregivers lose
track of the unique roles they play in a child's life. A new talker will
often call her caregiver "mommy," which makes parents worry that
their child is confused about who is who. She isn't. This is a case of
limited vocabulary rather than mixed-up identities. When a child has
only one word for the female person who takes care of her, her
calling both of them "mommy" is understandable.

Many parents become resentful and jealous of the amount of time
the caregiver spends with their child. They start feeling that their
child no longer belongs to them. Some parents become jealous of
"stylistic differences." Others may lose track of the fact that they are
the most important people in their child's life, and needlessly worry
that their child measures their love for her by what special activities
they do, or by how much time they spend with her every day. These
misplaced concerns set the stage for a long struggle with jealousy in
their relationship with a caregiver.

Feelings of jealousy can become the most undermining factor in
the relationship between parents and caregivers. Unchecked, jealousy will constantly eat away at your relationship.

When you are jealous of each other, your focus changes from how
you can best work together to which person your child likes better.
It is hard to see each other clearly and acknowledge how much you
each give your child. Here are some examples of how jealousy can
cause you to lose your perspective.

Coming home to see her baby in the arms of another person was
difficult enough for one mother. That her son was too young to
acknowledge her or her presence when she came home made her

more jealous. This jealousy pushed the mother to wish that she had hired a caregiver whom her son would not like, and who would be a bad caregiver as well—circumstances that were obviously not in the best interest of her son. But by the time her child turned five months old he would smile and reach for his mother when she came in. His natural development allowed his mother to be more secure and less jealous.

Allison, a caregiver, loved to do vigorous movements with the older children when they played outdoors. Keith, one of the children in her charge, loved to run and jump into her arms and be swept up into the air. His mother didn't have the energy or the desire to play with Keith so physically, and because she was unable to realize that children don't want or need their parents and caregivers to be clones of each other, she was worried that Keith was happier when he was with Allison than when he was with her. Her jealousy prevented her from seeing that Keith's life was being enriched by another adult.

Jealousy can also cause an underlying tension of ownership to emerge between parents and caregivers. Overprotectiveness and overpossessiveness can unbalance your relationship. Situations are created in which parents might ask "Whose child is it anyway?"

A caregiver's perfume was an overwhelming reminder for a mother that someone else was caring for her child. The mother would pick her child up every day and find him smelling like the caregiver's perfume. She couldn't stand it. She felt as if her child did not belong to her and she saw the caregiver's perfume as standing between her and her child. She would bathe her child immediately when they got home in order to reestablish *her* ownership. Her jealousy was never resolved.

Another mother had a caregiver who at times seemed to go beyond the limits of "professional caring." If the mother reported to the caregiver that the child had been sick during the night, the caregiver responded by saying she wished *she* could have been there for the child, as if she were the only person who could really take care of his needs.

But some relationships between parents and caregivers don't seem to be so threatened by jealousy. Some parents are able to set their jealous feelings aside to make room for another perspective. They are able to see that by including another adult in their child's life, they are enlarging her world within the security of their own relationship with the caregiver. They are giving her the opportunity to have a caring and trusting, but different, relationship with another adult.

One mother thought of her caregiver as a *friend* she was giving her son. Another mother appreciated the different cultural environment her caregiver was providing her son: "He feels her culture. I think he's a bit Salvadoran. He thinks in Spanish. He makes up dramatic plays in Spanish. His favorite is 'El Restaurante El Bundo,' which is about a tortilla restaurant." A third mother had a very practical approach to dealing with her feelings. "I haven't felt jealous. There have been times Jeremy has fallen and turned to Mrs. Turner, who takes care of him every day, even when I am there. But what can you expect if your child spends more time with his caregiver?"

☐ *Feelings of Guilt*

Guilt about sharing care is another common feeling that most parents will encounter at one time or another. They find themselves raising their children very differently from the way they were raised. These differences generate feelings of guilt, often expressed by a show of concern and worry about what *could be* if they were at home, or what *might not be* because they aren't at home. They feel guilty and worry about the amount of time that they have to spend with their children and about the quality of that time. They worry and feel guilty about what they are missing as parents by having their child in child care. And they worry about the effects of child care on their children.

Here are some examples of the sort of guilt some parents feel about their child care.

One mother felt guilty because her son had to conform to her schedule. She felt it made his schedule too rigid. She also felt that her schedule didn't allow them enough time in the day for hanging out together, no time for "free thinking," as she put it. She felt that if she were a stay-at-home mom instead, their time together would be less rushed and more spontaneous. She worried that over the long term such rigidly structured days would crush her child's imagination.

A toddler's parents felt guilty because they thought having their child in child care was putting him at an educational disadvantage. He was one of the two older children in a group of ten and his parents thought he was spending too much time doing "baby things." They felt that if they were home with him, they would be able to provide activities better suited to his age and abilities.

The mother of a two-year-old chose to go back to work, not for the money but because she wanted to. She felt she was a better mother because having her own life apart from her child helped her to be a more satisfied and happy person. But when her son cried in the morning as she left for the office she still worried about her decision.

Feelings of guilt can make parents act in ways that almost deny that their children are even being cared for by someone else. Joe's parents dashed in and out of the child-care program as quickly as they could, as if they needed to avoid seeing Joe and Kimberly, his caregiver, together. They spoke to Kimberly only when it was absolutely necessary. When Kimberly was on vacation, they were unable to introduce themselves to her substitute. Trying to deny the reality that Joe is in child care cancelled out any opportunity for them to get to know his caregivers and the program. Their darting in and out made it difficult for Kimberly and the other caregivers to approach them and begin building a relationship. And Joe can suffer.

Some parents take their guilty feelings out on their child's caregiver. Lottie's parents fit into this category. They often yelled at their caregiver for minor mistakes. They felt painfully guilty about having to leave their daughter in child care and would stay home with her if they could. When their caregiver lost one of Lottie's bottle caps they told her they didn't think she could do *anything* right. It's little wonder that the caregiver tiptoed around Lottie and her parents and that their communication with one another almost totally shut down.

Other parents bend over backward to make everything smooth in an attempt to assuage their guilt. Their relationship with their caregiver takes on an artificial quality. They are always trying to please their caregiver and never question her. A lopsided relationship like this isn't good for anyone, either.

Guilt isn't reserved for parents whose children are in child care. A mother who stayed home to care for her children sheds a different light on feelings of guilt. For those parents who feel guilty because they may miss special moments in their children's lives, she points out that she may not have been there, either: "I was home with my five children and I'm not sure I saw each one's first steps. They may well have taken their first steps when they were alone." And for parents who think they aren't taking good care of their children because they have them in child care, this mother shares her doubts about the quality of her *own* care: "My life was tough. There were days I was so tired I wondered if I was taking good care of my kids."

□ *Feelings of Resentment*

Resentment is a feeling even the most dedicated caregivers experience at one time or another. The reasons are many. Low salaries top the list. The National Child Care Staffing Study conducted by the Child Care Employee Project found that the predominantly female workforce of caregivers earns an average hourly wage of $5.35. Working conditions are high on the list, too, along with the lack of respect granted caregivers in this society.

As strange as it sounds, some caregivers may resent parents for placing their children in child care. Some caregivers may look upon the parents as adults who have abandoned their children. They take on the role of rescuer of these "abandoned" waifs. They start referring to a certain child as "my child" or want to take children home with them and care for them all the time. They begin to see parents as nuisances and obstacles to the care of the child. A caregiver who feels this way will clearly find it difficult to support a child's relationship with her parents. The relationship between caregiver and parent becomes one of "us" versus "them," the antithesis of what children need.

Caregivers can feel resentful of parents' occupations. They may feel envious of parents who make so much more money than they do working at jobs that appear so much more glamorous. Even the fact that a parent drops off her child and walks out the door to spend her day with other adults can be a source of resentment for the caregiver who feels she has been left behind to change diapers and wipe noses. A caregiver's resentment about a parent's employment can make it impossible for her to see how difficult it is for a mother or father to juggle two careers. Her resentment won't allow her to empathize with a parent or recognize how much a parent gives her child.

Resentment about salaries and poor working conditions also leads to a high turnover rate in the child-care field. Staff turnover has nearly tripled in the last decade, jumping from 15 percent in 1977 to 41 percent in 1988. Turnover has tremendous impact on a child's child-care experience and affects the relationship between parents and caregivers. A father, talking about the turnover in his son's child-care center, put it succinctly: "After a while, why bother getting to know and care for someone if she is just going to leave?" If the father feels that way, imagine how his child, who needs consistency in child care, feels.

What's Your Attitude?

In the preceding chapter we explained the necessity for parents and caregivers to have respect for themselves and their respective roles.

Now we want to emphasize the importance of respecting *each other*. Working together will be very awkward and uncomfortable if your attitudes toward each other are *dis*respectful, while seeing and respecting each other as whole people will enrich the lives of everyone involved.

What's *your* attitude toward your child's caregiver? What's *her* attitude toward you? How do you act toward her? How does she act toward you? Is either of you condescending, judgmental, impatient, or resentful? Or does your relationship reflect qualities of kindness, caring, and understanding?

Showing respect can easily be part of your daily life. Taking some time to develop personal rapport—to get to know each other as people—goes a long way in making your relationship work. It's one thing to talk about your child. It's another to pause for a moment and talk to each other about yourselves. Exchanging views about a movie, tales of a weekend trip to the beach, or just asking "How was your day?" helps you both remember that you have lives outside caring for the child.

Showing respect can be as simple as saying good morning to each other. It only takes a second no matter how hurried you are, or how busy a caregiver is. One caregiver made sure she always greeted children and parents when they walked in. But her greeting went beyond, "Hello, how are you?" Every day she carefully planned something to put on the center table, such as stamps or a bunch of flowers, so that everyone was greeted with something new to invite their interest and welcome their presence. In another, less thoughtful center, caregivers were so busy chatting with one another they didn't even notice when parents and children came in.

Having a caring attitude also reflects respect for the other person. A caregiver took three days off from work when her grandfather died. It was a hard time for her. The day she came back to work was difficult. One mother brought her a bunch of daisies. This meant a lot to the caregiver. You can do similar things for your caregiver. Ask her if her own child is over her cold. Notice her new haircut. She will appreciate the attention you give her.

Likewise, you will be pleased when she asks how things went with your presentation at work, or when she offers another quick way of cooking chicken for dinner, when she opens the door for you as you struggle out the door juggling your child, stroller, briefcase, and diaper bag, or when she makes sure you take home the special picture your child painted for you that day. One mother related that during a period when her family was going through a particularly rough time—her husband had been laid off and her sick mother had just moved in with them—her child's caregiver would have a cup of tea ready for her when she went to pick up her son. This concern and kindness was unexpected but sincerely appreciated.

Consider workable ways to improve your own caregiver's salary and/or working conditions. One father, speaking about his children's at-home caregiver, says, "I just try to put myself in her spot. If I was her, I wouldn't want to be dumped on. Working in a factory I know what that's like. For all the work she does, I can't pay her enough. But if I have the day off, I give her the day off with pay. I think she stays because I treat her fairly and respectfully."

Your help with small tasks—putting chairs up on the table, stacking blocks on the shelf, gathering dress-ups that are scattered across the room—shows you appreciate your caregiver's work, and will be welcomed. Acknowledging her effort in hanging new pictures on the wall gives recognition to her work. An occasional small gift that the caregiver will enjoy—a pineapple to cut up and serve for a snack, a bunch of flowers, a new book to read to the children—can brighten her day. Gifts are not necessary but they say loudly and clearly, "You and your work are special."

Having respect for each other also means that you can speak directly to each other, no matter what the issue. You don't have to use your child as a go-between. If, for example, you are annoyed that another pair of your child's socks is missing, say to the caregiver, "I'm upset. This is the second pair of socks that we've lost." This is much more honest and easier to deal with than saying coyly to your six-month-old in the caregiver's presence, "We have to tell Jenny to be more careful with your socks."

The same holds true for your caregiver. Asking you to please remember to bring in a new supply of diapers is more effective than for her to say to your toddler in front of you, "Remind Daddy to bring more diapers tomorrow."

And, of course, saying thank you acknowledges your appreciation of each other's efforts. There will be many times you help each other. Whether a caregiver helps you figure out a pattern to your child's temper tantrums or you volunteer some time to come and play your violin, a "thank you" is in order.

But showing respect is not so easy for some people. See for yourself in the following situations how the attitudes reflected by the parents' and caregivers' actions automatically put up barriers between them.

When a new mother told the caregiver that her four-month-old child had been throwing up when she fed her, the caregiver asked if the child had been burped and the mother responded that she had burped her once. The caregiver then reprimanded the mother and questioned her competency. In the words of the caregiver, "Once is not enough. Babies need to be burped more often. I thought *all* mothers knew that."

Another mother strolled into child care and announced that her child had dirty diapers but she wasn't going to change her because it was the caregiver's job.

A father, toddler, and caregiver were attending a country auction together. The father bought his child a hot dog, but neglected to ask if the caregiver might like one too. After the child had taken a bite of the hot dog and left it a slobbery mess, the father suggested the child share the hot dog with her caregiver. The caregiver declined in disgust.

Lack of respect for your caregiver can have its consequences. It's not that the caregiver is going to harm your child because you show her no respect, but caregivers, like everyone else, find it easier to do a little extra for children whose parents treat her with respect. They're more likely to have an extra reservoir of patience and understanding for a child whose parents show their appreciation by bringing in a snack, or pitching in at the end of the day to wipe off a few tables and stack a few chairs, than for parents who never give them the time of day.

Why are some people respectful and others less so? Who knows? Everyone has off days. But being disrespectful day in and day out will significantly lessen the ability of you and the caregiver to work together successfully. Respecting each other helps. And this respect must be genuine. You can't fake it in this or any other relationship. Your tone of voice, the words you choose, the expression on your face, and even your posture will give you away.

How You Can Communicate

Your separate roles as parent and caregiver serve as sources for different kinds of information about your child. As the parent, you know all your child's idiosyncrasies and what's happening at home, while your caregiver knows about kids in general and what's happening in child care. Some of this information is practical and some of it is quite frivolous. Some of the information is easy to share, some is more difficult. *All* of it is important. As you work together, find ways to share it.

☐ *What to Share*

Sharing news from home is a way you can influence your child's day even when you're at work. Information a caregiver has about your child's day can help you plan your evening at home. Knowing if your child is sleepy, hungry, excited, or upset about something, or news about her most recent accomplishments or setbacks, can help each of you plan your time together with her.

You can, for example, organize your plans around a child's need for sleep. Knowing that John woke up five times during the night means a caregiver will be alert to his "I'm tired" sign of rubbing his eyes, and offer him an earlier-than-usual morning nap. A caregiver can take a carriage to the park so Barry, who also had a restless night, can rest or ride home in it if he begins to fall apart after a morning of fishing in puddles. Knowing your child didn't take a nap might help you decide to skip the planned shopping trip for her new shoes and go home for an early dinner and bedtime instead.

Knowing when your child last ate gives you some idea of when she might be hungry. Though the snack is usually around ten o'clock, knowing that Ben missed breakfast because his family overslept means his caregivers can offer him something to eat. Discovering your child didn't eat lunch means you might be able to ward off the crankiness of hunger on your trip home by filling up her bottle on your way out the door, or offering her a snack of fruit before leaving child care.

Exchanging information about your child's newest interests and skills means you can give her the opportunity to practice them at home and in child care. Knowing that last night Peter drank out of a cup for the first time means his caregiver can offer him a cup at lunch. Hearing that Randy spent a lot of time in the bathroom watching three other two-year-olds sitting on the toilet in child care encourages Randy's parents to begin talking to him about using the potty, and to put a potty seat in the bathroom at home.

The information you share can help your child connect her worlds of home and child care—even if your child is cared for at home. Hearing that Ronny scrubbed carrots at snack time means his father can create a link with child care by talking about the prickly vegetable brush Ronny used, or by inviting him to help scrub potatoes for dinner. A Monday morning conversation with Tina's mother about the cat getting stuck in a tree gives Ginger, a caregiver, important information she can use in helping Tina feel close to her mother while they are separated.

"Look," says Ginger, pointing to a picture of a cat. "There's a kitty cat just like Tippy."

"Tippy climb tree," says Tina.

"Your mommy told me about that. Tippy climbed up in the tree and couldn't get down, right?"

Tina smiles broadly, listening to the story of the weekend's big event. "Then your mommy had to get a ladder and climb up to get Tippy."

"Mommy ladder," Tina says. "Tippy tree."

You can gain insight into a child's feelings by sharing information. You can understand why she might be acting unlike herself, why she might be whinier or quieter than normal. You can approach this unusual behavior differently than you would if you had no explanation for it. Your support for her can be directed to the cause of her distress.

When Jerry's sister was unexpectedly hospitalized, his routine at home was disrupted. Knowing this fact helped caregivers understand why Jerry got so upset when another child took his toy and why he couldn't relax and fall asleep at naptime. To support him during this period, they decided to give him some individual time with his special caregiver. They took a few walks alone, they made a snack together, and she helped him draw pictures to take to his sister.

Peggy was more fussy than usual when her father picked her up. Knowing that her favorite caregiver, Ellen, was home sick for the day guided Peggy's father to include the caregiver in their afternoon exchange. He talked about Ellen and Peggy, and they spent time looking at the picture of Ellen that hung on the side of the refrigerator. The information enabled him to respond to what Peggy might be feeling rather than just to her contrary behavior.

Sharing frivolous information adds another dimension to the relationship between you and your caregiver, and to what you both know about your child. Sharing stories about what your child says and does, stories that reveal the wonder of children and a little about how they see their world, can bring pleasure to both of you. You'll miss a lot if you and your caregiver don't share stories like these:

As a child crunched carrots for lunch he said, "Listen to my head."

As a two-year-old girl watched her father polish shoes she said, "I can smell brown."

As a child was showing a seed he found on the floor to a caregiver, she asked him if it were an orange seed and he replied that no, it's a *white* seed.

As a maintenance man replaced ceiling tiles a child announced that a new sky was being hung.

There can be difficulty in sharing information but it usually does not come from the information per se. Sometimes it's the language itself. Michelle and her husband, Leon, hired a woman who spoke only French, a language neither of them knew, to care for their son. They couldn't be clear about details ranging from what time she should bring Jason home from the park to what days she was working and what Jason ate that day for lunch. Not being able to speak to their child's caregiver literally cut them off from their son's care. Not being able to understand one another, it was impossible for them to share any kind of information.

Difficulties also arise when simple, clear-cut information such as how much a child slept or ate is overlaid with feelings of self-doubt and worry. These are some of the hardest situations.

A toddler's parents wonder what is wrong with *them* when they can't get their child to sleep through the night. Another mother knows her daughter has her wrapped around her little finger when it comes to eating. If she offers her daughter an apple, she wants an orange, and the minute she finishes peeling the orange, she wants a sandwich. The mother is worried that her daughter doesn't eat enough and that *she* has made a mess out of her diet. Parents are afraid that sharing this kind of information will be a bad reflection on their parenting.

Caregivers also worry about sharing certain information. It's hard to explain to parents that some days you can be creative and some days you can't, or that there are days when you are angry and frustrated, without being concerned that this information will be taken the wrong way or that you will be perceived as a bad caregiver.

But sharing information doesn't mean you have to bare your soul to a caregiver. It takes time to feel enough trust in another person to share what is important to you, and there may be some things you will never want to share. There may be some things about your child you haven't even articulated for yourself. *What* you need to share includes:

- What was your child's evening at home like?
- Is there anything unusual about her daily routines?
- Are there any changes in her health? Anything to watch out for such as a new cough or the beginning of a diaper rash?
- Is she working on any new skills, such as eating with her fingers or beginning to brush her teeth?
- Is there anything out of the ordinary that might affect her, such as a parent being away on a business trip, a visit from her grandparents, a new pet at the child-care center?
- Is there anything your child has done that has made you laugh that your caregiver would enjoy hearing about?

□ *When, Where, and How to Share It*

The morning and the end of the day are usually the times you have to talk with each other, which means many of your conversations are held on the run. It's difficult to have an extended discussion in the midst of wrestling with a stuck zipper on your child's snowsuit, helping her say good-bye, or gathering her wet clothes, empty bottles, and paintings for the trip home. Don't despair. It's amazing how much communication can take place in bits and snatches over time.

Sometimes someone else—an older sibling, relative, or housekeeper—may drop your child off in the morning and pick her up in the afternoon. Though you and your child's caregiver might not see each other for weeks, you still need to communicate with each other.

Let the caregiver know who will be dropping off or picking up your child in your place. Provide your substitute with questions to ask, information to share with the caregiver, and information to bring home. And make sure you check in with the caregiver by phone at least once a week.

Written communication—a note from home, a bulletin board where caregivers post the news of the day, daily reports a parent fills out in the morning and the caregiver fills out in the afternoon—is no replacement for talking, but it can help fill in some gaps. Putting pen to paper can keep communication flowing when you don't see each other.

Some caregivers ask parents to fill out a sheet each morning with daily news. This assures that caregivers will remember important details that can easily be forgotten, especially in a group setting. A written record means that a caregiver who works the afternoon shift can have the same information as the morning caregiver.

Some programs ask parents to write weekly about their child's current activities. This is good to do even when your child is cared for at home. These written communications track your child's development. And if you save them you'll have a great record of your child's first years that you and she will enjoy in years to come.

The phone can be useful for extended conversations and for talking more privately with your caregiver. It's especially useful when the subject of the conversation is your child and not the news of the day, because young children, even those who do not yet speak a word, know when they are being talked about and are quick to sense the tone of what you are saying.

In addition to sharing information in the classroom and over the phone, there will be times you need to arrange a conference where you can sit down face to face. Conferences can be about any subject. Their topic can be as general as comparing notes about what your child is up to, or as specific as focusing on toilet training, separation, biting, or sibling rivalry.

Some child-care programs regularly schedule two conferences a year, with the idea that if you need more they can be scheduled.

Arranging conferences is a good idea even with a private caregiver. Though you see each other every day, a conference gives you a structured time to focus on your child. You should each have time to prepare, to think about what you are going to say, to collect anecdotes and observations.

Because of the somewhat formal nature of conferences—their resemblance to "being called into the principal's office"—parents and caregivers often feel nervous about conferences, so it can be helpful to assure that conferences are just another time to exchange information. You can also make your conferences special, as these parents did:

We've had the same caregiver for five years. At the beginning of each new year we have a special dinner with her. We get the silver out, a tablecloth, and have a good bottle of wine. We treat her as a special guest, rather than as part of the family. My husband and I cook dinner. We review the year and look ahead to the next one. We ask her what her plans are. Is she planning to be with us for the whole year? We want to check in and see how things are going for her. Is she happy? Bored? Is there anything we can do to make things better? We talk about the kids. We have a few laughs. It's the time we give her a yearly raise, too.

Continuing communication keeps the doors open between you and your child's caregiver. You are supporting your child as you enrich your view of her. Talking together about everyday events gives you practice in communicating with each other that will be helpful in resolving inevitable conflicts.

This brings us to a source of many conflicts: being on time at the end of the day.

□ *Can You Be on Time?*

Why is being on time treated in this chapter of the book? Simple: Being late is one of the easiest and most common ways to uninten-

tionally upset your relationship with your caregiver. Being on time is
more than just a matter of minutes.

Your being on time at the end of the day is an often undiscussed
yet assumed part of the "contract" between you and your child's
caregiver. When you break the contract, feelings of anger and resentment build. So be clear about *what* is closing time. Remember
that it takes time for your child to say hello to you, to gather her
belongings, and to say good-bye to the caregiver. Arrive at least ten
to fifteen minutes before your program closes so you are walking out
the door before closing time.

There are times when being late is unavoidable, and caregivers
understand this. If you find you are going to be late, call ahead. Let
your child-care provider know you will be delayed and for how long.
When you arrive apologize and thank the caregiver for helping you
out.

There may also be times you think, "What's five minutes?" You
decide to stop for a newspaper, to chat with a friend on the way out
of the office, or to walk the final block to your child's child-care
program slowly, trying to unwind a bit from work and to gear up for
the rest of the evening. You justify being late; you have so little time
for yourself, you are paying a lot for child care, and, anyway, the
caregiver will still be there talking to another parent or two. How
much could five minutes matter?

They matter a lot to your caregiver. Regardless of how much she
enjoys being with your child, at the end of the day she is eager to be
off duty. She's ready to get on with her personal life and your being
late encroaches upon her personal time. The five minutes you added
to your life have just taken five away from hers.

Therefore, when you are late you probably will not be greeted
warmly. Information you want and need at the end of a long day will
not be forthcoming. Instead, you might find your child and caregiver
dressed in their coats, sitting on the bench outside the door, or find
your child walking around the room empty-handed because all the
toys have been put away on the shelf—signals caregivers often use to
say "You are late."

PART · THREE

Working Together

You have chosen a mode of child care, perhaps even made specific arrangements. You have thought carefully about the differing roles of parent and caregiver. Now you are ready for the real world, for that day when you leave your child in the care of someone else for the first time. You are ready to put theory into practice.

But how do you work together with your caregiver if you're ten miles apart? How do you work together with your caregiver if both of you are in the same room? What kind of support does your child need, and how much of that support can you, a working parent, realistically give? This section will help you answer those questions, and it is based on one premise: Your child probably needs more support than you may think she needs; however, she does not require more than you are capable of giving her.

Chapter 7

Beginning Child Care

Think of a time when you began something new: attending a new school, perhaps an adult-education class, or starting a new job. How did you feel? Happy? Excited? Nervous? Proud? Scared? Any new and important experience always evokes mixed feelings. Even as adults, we have to figure out who is who, how things work, how we feel about this place, these people, and this activity before we settle in and feel comfortable. So it should not surprise or concern you when your child requires time to settle into child care. This chapter will take a look at how children, caregivers, and parents can make the first few weeks of child care a good experience for everyone.

The First Days

Ideally, children's schedules for their entry into child care should be individualized. If you have a private caregiver, you and the caregiver can plan a personal schedule. Child-care programs usually send out notices about the beginning schedule. Obviously, these can't be individualized. But even if you have an individualized schedule, keep in mind that the maturity and unique temperament of your child will determine how easily and quickly she'll adjust. The most individualized schedule is still an artificial structure imposed upon a child by adults.

Gradual entry to child care is recommended. Infants and toddlers should begin spending a few hours at a time with their new caregiver or in their new program, gradually increasing their hours over the first few weeks. It takes a lot of energy for your child to be with new people or to be in a new place. Gradual entry allows your child to adjust to her new situation without getting overly tired or overly stimulated. She can experience new people and new things when she is at her best.

For the first few days, you should plan to stay with your child the entire time, if at all possible. After a few days, you and the caregiver may decide it is time for you to begin leaving your child alone. Plan to stay close by and return shortly. Then increase your time away bit by bit until your child is spending the day without you.

Your schedule will need to fit into the child-care entry schedule, but the reality is that you may not be able to accomplish this. Many employers don't allow parents time to get their children settled into child care. You may have one hour, or maybe one morning. Perhaps you can arrange to take personal leave time. Depending on your situation, it may be possible to talk to your boss and explain, "I am a valuable worker here. I will be a better worker if I have some time to help my child get settled into child care so I don't have to spend all day worrying about her."

Your schedule might not allow for you to be there at all. If this is the case, consider asking someone your child knows—a relative or neighbor—to spend time with her. If that's not possible, there are still other options open to you to help your child start child care. A private caregiver could spend time with your family in the evening or on a weekend; a caregiver from a program could visit your home.

Getting to Know the Place

It's up to both you and the caregiver to help your child get to know her child-care setting. If your child is being cared for in another space, the caregiver needs to orient you to the new space. And if the caregiver is working in your home, she needs some guidance from you.

In family child care or a child-care center, your child will be getting to know an entirely new place. She will be learning the routine of the program and the space itself. She will encounter things she has never seen before, such as big cardboard blocks or a wooden rowing boat. For your infant, getting to know the child-care setting might mean becoming accustomed to a new changing table. Your toddler will be learning where the toys are, where the reading corner is, and when the group has its snack. Your two-year-old may be fascinated by the low sinks in the bathroom with faucets she can reach, or with playing hide-and-seek with a new friend.

Getting to know all these new things is a gradual process and happens within the normal routine of the program. The children will learn about their new space as the caregiver leads them through their daily activities. However, for these first few days *you* are there to help. You are there to participate in new experiences with your child, such as preparing a snack, listening to a story, or singing with a group. You are there to change her diapers for the first few days until she feels comfortable enough to allow the caregiver to change her. Your presence gives your child security and confidence in her new setting and makes it easier for her to settle in.

And, of course, you too will have to settle into this new space—with the assistance of the caregiver, ideally. She may welcome you grandly: a pot of hot water for making tea and coffee says loudly and clearly, "Come in and stay awhile." She may make a poster featuring a list of parents', children's, and caregivers' names that can make it easier to figure out who belongs with whom. She can help you find your way around by labeling drawers so you can find the paper cups, or by showing you where to hang your coat and bag when you come for a visit or where the peanut butter is for emergency snacks.

This settling-in period is also the time for you to inquire about the child-care center's vacation schedule and to make alternative plans for those days. Having to lose a day of work unexpectedly or scramble to find someone to care for your child at the last minute is not good for you or your child. Perhaps you can ask a neighbor or relative to care for your child on those days, arrange to work at home, or put aside a few vacation days. These alternatives can also be put into service when your child must stay home sick.

If your child is being cared for at home, she doesn't have to learn about a new place. But her caregiver does. Small things like having her favorite juice on hand are welcoming. Give her a tour of your house or apartment. Highlight things of special importance to your child, such as her crib, highchair, and toys. Show the caregiver where the things that she will need during the day are. Give her places to put her things. Show her the closet in which she may hang a coat. Help her feel at home by being clear about your arrangements. Is she bringing her lunch or are you providing it? Show her where cups, plates, and tea are in the kitchen. Explain any household quirks such as the answering machine or the noisy dishwasher.

Getting to know the place also means getting to know how you and your caregiver can share the same space. This process is a little different depending on whether your child is in child care or has a caregiver at home, but basically you're trying to help each other without getting in each other's way. Here are some suggestions for getting settled. You can put all of them to use immediately and use them throughout the year as well.

- Watch and listen to the caregiver for clues to how you may be best involved. When the caregiver announces that it's time to begin getting ready for lunch, complete the "jumping on the pillow" game you are playing with your toddler and her friend and steer them toward the bathroom to wash their hands.

- You, like any new adult in the setting, may disrupt daily routines. Starting to build a block tower may begin a group movement toward you. If the caregivers are trying to get the children ready for a walk around the neighborhood, your block building becomes a major, although unintentional, disruption.

- As you are beginning to learn about the setting, ask questions about how you can best participate. Is there a good place for you to be in the room? Is there an activity you could do with your child and perhaps a couple of others? Where should you put the paintings to dry? Ask the caregiver what you can do to help her. An extra helper sensitive to what is happening in the room is always welcome.

- Discuss how your visits will influence your child's daily schedule. Lunchtime is a popular visiting time. Yet your presence can make taking an after-lunch nap more difficult for your child. Why should she want to go to sleep when you are around? With a caregiver's help, you might develop a routine of reading a story with your child before you go back to the office and then letting the caregiver help her take a nap.

  If your child is cared for at home, know what time your caregiver puts your child down for a nap so you can conveniently check in with her while your child is asleep.

- Be aware that adult talking can be disruptive. Follow the caregiver's lead as to how much she can talk with you. If things are slow, she may be happy for some grown-up company. On the other hand, carrying on a conversation may disrupt the focus she needs. Talking with other parents can be tricky because your child will naturally want your attention when you are there. If she is occupied and you can visit with other parents, keep the volume down so you don't disrupt what is going on.

  Your child will also want your attention when you arrive home from work. Don't be surprised if your child doesn't let you speak to your at-home caregiver until you have spent some time with her first.

- Sit down whenever possible. This prevents your child and the others from feeling that a giant is now in their presence, and it makes you more available to them. But a word to the wise: Look before you sit. Toys, small pieces of crayon or chalk, a little mud from outside, something unidentifiable but sticky—any one of these could be in the spot you have picked to sit.

- Make life as easy as you can for everyone by taking care of the details of daily routines. Label your child's clothes and possessions so you know what belongs to whom. Organize supplies so you and the caregiver can focus on your child and not spend so much time looking for missing things. Find out where to put your child's changes of clothes, her diapers, and her lunch, if you supply them. Provide supplies you are asked to bring or make sure you have enough supplies at home. Being sure that there are enough diapers to last through the day, or that your child has a blanket for naptime, makes the caregiver's life much easier. Take care of tasks that are part of the routine, such as washing your child's sheet weekly or supplying a snack once a month. Let your at-home caregiver know if you are out of milk so she can plan a walk to the store before lunch.

- There are many ways you can be involved in your child's child-care program. Parents differ in how they want to be involved and how much time they have. You may have chosen a program in which you can serve on the board or head a committee, or you may want to participate in less time-consuming ways. Some programs expect parents to fulfill certain obligations, such as participating in two or three weekend workdays over the course of the year. Others leave it up to you. You may want to consider working on a newsletter, making phone calls to remind parents of meetings or other events, donating old clothes for the dress-up corner, repairing a broken toy, taking photographs, or sharing some of your own interests, such as playing the violin or folk dancing. One father in Vermont brings a baby lamb to the child care center from his farm each spring.

Getting to Know One Another

In private care and family child care there is one caregiver. Even in a center with several caregivers, your child will get to know one of them better than the others. That caregiver may be assigned to your child at the beginning of the year, or this choice may be left to "chemistry." In any event, child and caregiver will find each other. Your child's special caregiver is the one who knows your child especially well and can read what she is saying through her crying, gestures, babbling, and words. She is the person your child can depend on to be there with a word of encouragement when a puzzle piece just will not fit into place, and with a cheer when placing the last piece reveals the caterpillar. It's not that your child won't get to know the other caregivers. Rather, her special caregiver is the one she will run to for a hug or to share their silly song or joke. And just as she will be learning about her new space day by day, she will also gradually get to know her caregiver.

Your presence helps get the relationship between your child and the special caregiver off to a good start. Sitting on your lap or looking across the room and seeing you there allows your child to reach out and begin to acquaint herself with the new adult in her life. Even though you may feel silly sitting on a little chair or building blocks, your being there gives the caregiver and your child's relationship with her your seal of approval.

Your presence also allows you time to get to know the caregiver. It's a perfect opportunity to learn how the caregiver manages children in general, and specifically, how she relates to your child. You can listen to the tone of her voice, and observe how she disciplines children and how she handles them physically.

Your caregiver will learn about your child gradually, but to help your child settle into child care as best she can, the caregiver needs a head start. Sharing information was discussed in a previous section, but these first few days are when this sharing *really* begins. Information you and the caregiver share with each other at this time will create a foundation to work from that will allow you both to feel more confident about the task at hand.

In some programs, a caregiver will interview you to obtain the information she needs. Others may give you a questionnaire to fill out. With her questions, she will try to obtain practical information from you about your child's daily routine. She will try to find out a little about the family and she will try to get a feel for your child. If you feel there is something a caregiver needs to know, now is the time to tell her.

Questions that your caregiver might ask at this time include:

- What is your child's daily schedule?
- When does she eat? Sleep? Play?
- Does she have health problems? Allergies?

- Does your child have any brothers or sisters?
- Who are the adults in the household?
- Do you have any pets? What kinds?

- What kinds of things does your child like to do? To eat?
- What are her favorite songs? Games? Books?
- What gets her upset? Noise? Darkness? Your leaving?
- How do you comfort her?

You should also ask questions, no matter how silly they may seem to you. A caregiver has information that can help you feel more at ease about leaving your child. You will probably have many practical questions about the program, will want to know about the child-care "family," and will want to get a feel for the caregiver. You could very simply reverse the caregiver's questions from the list above. Ask her when the children eat, sleep, and play. Ask who the other caregivers are in a child-care center, or who the other family members are in a family child-care program. Ask what the caregiver's favorite activities are to do with the children, her favorite children's books and songs, and how she comforts an upset child.

Some of these details may seem so basic you wonder why we would bother talking about them. But they are a vital part of giving the caregiver a picture of your child's life at home and giving you a picture of your child's life in child care. Lack of information about a child's unusual home created unnecessary anxiety for one caregiver we know. A toddler in her room had a funny gait. She and her coworker spent several hours trying to decide if they should refer the parents to an orthopedist. How would the parents react? Maybe it would be better not to upset them. But on the other hand, what if there was a problem that could be corrected if caught early enough? They decided to talk to the parents. As it happened, a few days before the conference was scheduled to take place, one of the caregivers visited the child at home—which turned out to be a houseboat! The toddler's gait reflected the rocking of his home. Knowing where this child lived would have saved these caregivers a lot of worry and perhaps an embarrassing conference with the parents had they not coincidentally made a home visit.

Reacting to the Newness

During this settling-in period you may notice some changes in your child's behavior at home and in child care. She may, for example, be more clingy than usual. It makes sense that if you are beginning to leave her, she will want to stay particularly close when you are around. Though your first response may be to discourage this behavior because you want to get on with the difficult task of learning to part from each other, resist it. Giving her the extra attention and contact she is asking for as she becomes your shadow will help nourish her when it comes time to say good-bye.

Don't be surprised if your child's sleep is disrupted. Sleeping is a kind of separation, and your child is already dealing with separating from you during the day. It can take a child time to feel comfortable enough to fall asleep in child care. On the other hand, she may cope with her initial unease by sleeping more than normal at home or at child care. She may not eat as much as usual, or she may be cranky. Such behavior is to be expected. It doesn't mean your child doesn't like child care.

But sometimes children respond in ways that indicate a child-care arrangement isn't working for them. It's normal for children to cry and get clingy or change their sleeping schedules as they settle into child care. But if over a period of weeks your child cannot get settled, if she cannot respond affectionately to her caregiver, it's time to examine the situation. Her response to child care doesn't mean that you or she have failed. It may simply mean that she has to grow up a little more or needs a different kind of setting.

□   □   □

Randy (eight months) began coming to the child-care program where his older brother had spent two happy years. He clung to his mother, never even looking up to see what was going on in the room. She was concerned, but she also had to get back to work. She talked with the caregiver, learned that some children require longer than others to feel comfortable in a new place, and decided to give him a few more weeks. Knowing that children at around eight months of age can be wary of new people, mother and caregiver made a plan. Randy's aunt would come and stay at the child-care center.

Every couple of days the mother and caregiver talked on the phone. Six weeks went by and there was no change. The caregiver had seen other children take as long to begin settling into child care, but she was aware that this child's behavior was telling her something. Because he never took a step away from his aunt or even looked around the room made her think that this wasn't the place for him. Again she talked with the mother, who felt that her child had somehow failed. The caregiver tried to explain that this wasn't the case at all. The mother then decided to have someone take care of Randy at home. The following year, older and wiser, he came back to the child-care center and had a terrific experience.

Whatever changes you see in your child's behavior, be certain to share them with the caregiver. Keeping in touch with each other about how your child is doing is one way you can assist her. Your child can't tell you in words how it's going for her so it's up to you to keep track.

Chapter 8

Hellos and Good-byes

There will be mornings when your child gives you a hug, waves good-bye, and turns to read a book with her caregiver, or joins other children building with blocks. There will be afternoons when you walk in the door and are greeted with a big hug and a hello kiss. But not always. There is no way to predict what will happen on any particular day.

Separation from and reuniting with loved ones are basic experiences of life for toddlers, teenagers, and adults. They are not problems to be solved. There is no "right" way to say hello and good-bye to your child. However, you can help make mornings and afternoons a little easier for everyone.

In this chapter we will look at the factors that affect your child's ability to say hello and good-bye, and your options for making the experience easier. We'll also make some suggestions for saying hello and good-bye each day. You may already do some of these things, but perhaps without realizing their importance. Others may be new ideas you'll want to try.

Why Hellos and Good-byes Can Be Difficult

If you and your child's caregiver look past your child's behavior, you won't be confused or shaken by the way your child handles separation. You will see that your child's age, events at home, her health, and even the day of the week have an effect on the way your child can say hello and good-bye. You will see that what appears to be totally random behavior often is not.

Around eight months of age, infants show how attached they are to their parents by becoming curious about strangers and often getting very upset when it is time to say good-bye to their parents. As emphasized throughout this book, every infant knows who is who in her life. Infants don't want to see the person they know and love best walking out the door.

Young toddlers just beginning to walk seem so busy practicing new skills—climbing up the slide, walking across the room, dumping a bucket full of blocks—that they hardly acknowledge your departure. Having just finished dealing with this same person when she was a clinging, crying infant, you may find yourself thinking, with a sigh of relief and some regret, that your toddler no longer needs you as much. It's not true. Though your leaving may seem simpler, she is still very aware of you. Touching base with you fuels her exploring. When you are not around she may be quieter than usual. At this age, your return is often marked by a sparkle in her eye and an increased energy level. It's as if she is recharged by your presence.

A few months later, the same child may again be clinging to you desperately, begging you not to leave. She has discovered that the world is a big place and she is quite small. She is aware in a new way how much she needs you. It makes sense that children aged eighteen to thirty months find it very difficult to say good-bye, and can protest strongly with clinging, kicking, and screaming. They can also protest by giving you the cold shoulder. When it comes time to say good-bye and your child becomes very busy trying to fit a puzzle piece into a space on the board, she isn't saying, "Go ahead. I don't care if you leave," as you might think. Rather, she is showing how difficult it is to say good-bye. By turning her attention elsewhere, *she* is leaving first.

You may get the same cool treatment in the afternoon as she takes charge of your greeting. It is as if she were telling you, "OK, we did it your way this morning. Now I'm calling the shots." One mother was confused and disturbed because on the same days that it was hard for her son to say good-bye in the morning, he wouldn't want to go home with her in the afternoon. He would dawdle until she had to carry him crying to the car. However, his dawdling was his way of taking control of the situation. It was a normal and healthy response.

As your child approaches three years of age, separation becomes relatively easier, although she *still* needs your help. She is better able to carry a sense of you with her when you are not there, and her language skills are more developed. Even on days when she does get upset saying hello or good-bye, her maturity makes comforting her easier, too.

Situations at home can affect saying hello and good-bye. Changes in daily routine, large and small, can make your child feel unsettled. Your being away on a business trip, an overnight guest in the house, an illness in the family, or a divorce can make it more difficult for your child to say good-bye and hello. She may be more clingy than usual, or lodge her protests more strongly than usual.

A child's health can affect saying hello and good-bye. When we are feeling good, we are all able to manage better than if we have even a simple cold, which can make children—and many adults too— more needy than usual.

The day of the week also influences the beginning and the end of the day. Hank's father describes the effect of weekends together on saying good-bye on Monday morning:

On Saturday and Sunday we are together all day long. We take time to make a real breakfast, we go to the post office and supermarket, hang out in the backyard. We get back in touch with each other. And then, too quickly, Monday morning comes. It's hard for Hank when we have to say good-bye at the child-care center door. He's more clingy than any other day of the week and usually cries. I know the feeling. By the middle of the week we're settled back into our routine and are looking forward to another weekend.

Making Hellos and Good-byes Easier

☐ *A Proper Good-bye*

It can be hard to say good-bye to someone you love. Your child is often crying and you and the caregiver feel like crying too. Sneaking out may become your way of saying good-bye.

On the surface, it may seem like the best thing to do. After all, if your child is happily listening to a story or drinking a cup of juice, why interrupt to say good-bye? You know she will probably end up protesting and crying anyway. A quiet exit can make things simpler for the caregiver, who doesn't have to comfort her, and might mean you can begin your own day tear-free. On the practical side, dealing with a crying child takes time, which is in limited supply.

But when we look through the eyes of your child, we see that what may seem better really isn't. Imagine how you would feel if you looked up from the blocks you were stacking or the fish you were helping feed to find that the person you depend on most in the world, one of your parents, had disappeared with no warning. Chances are, you would begin to feel as if you had to keep alert: if your mother or father can disappear so quickly, the world isn't such a safe place. What might happen next? When will they come back and when will they leave again? It would be difficult to relax even when they were there because you'd never be sure when they might vanish again.

Sneaking out is a betrayal of your child's trust in you. This is true even if your infant is too young to understand the word "good-bye," or your toddler is so busy rocking in the wooden rowboat she doesn't seem to care if you are there or not. Saying good-bye to your infant is an investment in the future. Over time she will come to recognize that your putting on your coat and walking to the door goes along with saying good-bye. By saying good-bye, you are telling her that she can trust you to tell her about what is going to happen. Your leaving is a big event in her life. No matter how busy your toddler may seem, she is very aware of you. Disappearing on her shakes her foundation and her relationship with you. As one caregiver explains to parents in her family child-care home, "Saying good-bye is worth it even if it costs some tears and time."

☐ *Listening to Tears*

It's hard to listen to any child crying. This is true for you and your child's caregiver. So you both try to help your child by stopping her crying. This becomes the focus of your best efforts. It's likely that some of your urgency to stop a child's crying is caused by the stirring up of your own childhood feelings about being left behind. Also, there are times when it's difficult to know how to comfort your child. You and her caregivers may feel frustrated and ineffective. You have to do something, so you try to stop her tears.

Simply stopping your child's crying doesn't necessarily address her tears. We make the assumption that crying means trouble. Actually, it is only natural that sometimes your child cries when you leave. Sometimes the children who need to be watched most closely are those who don't cry, because they don't yet feel *safe* enough to do so. When your child cries, she needs someone to listen to her, to respond to what she is saying, not a well-meaning adult who tries to stop her tears by waving a toy in front of her face or singing a silly "bouncing-on-the-knee" song.

We're not suggesting that you let her cry indefinitely. Sometimes your child may need encouragement to dry her tears and turn her attention to something else, such as reading a story or making play dough. But only after being listened to first.

Listening, really listening to a child crying is more than it appears to be. When you stop to listen to crying, you may be surprised at what you hear.

Tom (sixteen months) cries as his mother prepares to leave him with his caregiver in a neighborhood park.

The caregiver and her ten-year-old daughter, who serves as her helper when she's not in school, begin offering suggestions with the good intention of easing Tom's good-bye.

"Do you want to play on the slide?"

"Do you want to go to my house?"

Tom kicks at his stroller and continues fussing.

"Wait a minute," his mother says.

"What are you saying?" she asks Tom.

"Cookie subway."

"Fine," says his mother. "I'll give Marcy a quarter and you can stop to buy a cookie by the subway on your way to her house."

Tom nods, smiling now. His mother gives Marcy a quarter. She kisses him good-bye. He waves as she walks down the street.

As his mother explained, "Tom was snowed by helpfulness." Only by stopping and listening could his mother and caregiver understand that he had figured out his own way to deal with saying good-bye.

Children are resourceful and resilient. By listening to your child you are telling her she can feel anything from annoyance to delight in figuring out a strategy to say good-bye, and that no matter how strong and mixed her feelings are she will be all right and you will be there to help her. You are opening the world to her.

□ *Acknowledging They're Gone*

Sometimes caregivers believe it is better not to mention parents during the day because it is upsetting to children. Parents avoid talking about saying good-bye as if it doesn't happen. But children have feelings whether or not there is the opportunity to express them. Offering children the opportunity to express those feelings tells them they are not alone.

Rather than avoid the subject, caregivers can use specific language to surround children with their parents' presence during the day. Asking "Did you and Daddy come in the car this morning?" while taking a neighborhood walk and listening to a honking horn, or asking "Did your mommy tie that ribbon in your hair?" when helping the child change her wet shirt helps steep child care with the presence of the parents.

Responding to your child's comment, "Me cry," with the story of her tears that morning when you said good-bye can offer her the comfort of going through the experience again at a distance. This is different from "laying" your feelings on your child. We're not suggesting that every time a child is upset caregivers say, "You must be missing your mommy or daddy." Or that you spend all your time together with your child talking about the time when you're apart. But separation is part of life. It is there whether or not you talk about it. So you should at least acknowledge it.

☐ *Getting It Together*

Saying hello and good-bye demands organization. Being organized, to the extent possible when living or working with children under three, means you and the caregiver can focus on your child during morning and afternoon transitions when she needs your help. A few moments spent the night before packing supplies (extra diapers, a change of clothes), checking clothes for missing buttons and broken zippers before you lay them out, packing lunches, or being sure there is enough milk or apple juice to fill morning bottles can remove some of the tension involved in getting out of the house in the morning.

Caregivers can save you time and avoid frustration and sore knees from crawling under cribs or behind toy shelves by designating a place to put empty bottles during the day, so you can find them in the afternoon. Labeling children's clothes and other objects can greatly simplify gathering your child's belongings at the end of the day. For a few dollars, you can buy a nonwashable laundry marker. It's a worthwhile item for the little hassles it can help you avoid.

Saying Hello and Good-bye

☐ *A Time of Transitions*

Child-care mornings and afternoons are transition times for parents, caregivers, and children. They necessitate moving from place to place, either for you and your child or for your caregiver. They demand that everyone make adjustments to new situations. And they revolve around those moments of saying hello and good-bye.

For children, hellos and good-byes in child care are twofold. Saying hello to her caregiver means your child will soon be saying good-bye to you. Greeting you at the end of the day signals it will soon be time to say good-bye to her caregiver. Your child must adjust from being with you to being with her caregiver in the morning, and back to being with you at the end of the day.

For parents, getting to a child-care program can be a feat involving juggling briefcase, diaper bag, carseat, and baby. Being certain everyone is dressed and lunches are packed is only the prelude to getting out the door and on your way to child care.

Once you arrive at child care, or, in the case of a private caregiver, once she arrives at your home, your child needs your help to say hello, connect with her caregiver, and settle in for the day. Even though you may be thinking ahead to the papers on your desk or customers waiting for you at your next stop, your child needs a final few minutes of your attention.

Even if you don't have much time—and who does?—you can make the most of it. Taking off your coat, which takes only a few seconds, says to your child, "I'm here with you." Whatever your morning routine is—reading a short story, putting your child's lunch away in the refrigerator, or sitting at the table with other parents and children for a cup of milk—be there for your child. If your child is cared for at home, the same principle holds true. Take a moment to sit on the couch with her and her caregiver as you talk about the day ahead.

Pat tells about bringing his sixteen-month-old daughter Rachel to her child-care program. "I was on edge. I dreaded leaving. What would I do if she started to cry? I didn't have that much time so we spent our ten minutes standing in the middle of the room, Rachel clinging to my coat, preparing for the worst. Talk about being uncomfortable."

Betty, Rachel's caregiver, shares her impression of what was happening: "I'd see them standing there. It was painful. After ten minutes or so, Pat would say good-bye and leave as soon as he could pull his coat away from Rachel, who by then was usually crying hard. It was clear something was not working for either of them, so Pat and I talked. I suggested that Pat use the same ten minutes to read a book with Rachel."

Pat continues, "Anything was better than what was happening, so the next morning I took off my coat. Rachel and I sat down on the big blue pillows in the reading corner and I read her a story. We were both more relaxed. My settling in meant Rachel could begin settling in when I was there. She still cried sometimes, but it was different. I felt like I could help her a little and that she knew I was there for her."

If you are on a tight, early morning schedule, you might ask if you can come a few minutes early so you can spend a few minutes with your child. This may or may not work for your child's caregiver. With such long hours every day, caregivers have little time to organize materials and make plans for the day. Your caregiver may allow you to come early if you agree to be solely responsible for your child. But she may also consider her quiet time before the program opens precious. If it's not convenient for your caregiver to let you in early, perhaps you can read a story together in the car as you wait for the center to open.

Finally, there is the moment of actually saying good-bye. A few minutes before you have to leave, give your child a warning, even if you believe she is too young to understand what you are saying. Because she is just beginning to develop a concept of time, give her something concrete to help her understand the meaning of "soon" or "in five minutes." You might say, "Daddy has to go to the office as soon as we finish this book," or "Mommy is going to work after you climb up the slide two more times."

Your child is not the only one you should inform. Cue in a care-giver so she can be available to help your child say good-bye to you. Knowing you are leaving means the caregiver can finish diapering another child or mixing up juice, and pay attention to your child. It is nice for your child to have her caregiver there when you leave. You will feel better knowing the caregiver is available to comfort your child or, if necessary, help her move into an activity. The care-giver will feel more effective.

Catch her eye or say "I'm going to go in a minute. Will you be able to help Becky if she needs it?" If a caregiver is busy, wait a few moments before you leave. Remember that if your child is in a group setting, you are saying good-bye to her only, while a caregiver may be trying to help several children and parents say good-bye. If you are running late and need to leave immediately, alert the caregiver so she can arrange to be close by if your child needs her.

After you say good-bye, it is generally not a good idea to come back into the room. It's confusing for your child and often for the caregiver. It's not a hard-and-fast rule—of course there may be times when you want to or need to step back in—but not returning makes your leaving more predictable for your child. You can still check to see how she is doing if she was upset when you left. You may listen at the door until you hear your child stop crying. Some centers have one-way windows through which you may observe your child stepping into her day. Ask that a caregiver stick her head out the door to tell you everything is all right. Or call when you get to work.

Reuniting in the afternoon also requires some planning. Allow enough time to help your child reconnect to you *and* to get ready for your trip home. If possible, allow a few minutes to join your child in what she is doing. Imagine how you would feel if you were suddenly swept out of a place and away from people you had been with all day. Arriving ten or fifteen minutes (or more if possible) before your child's program closes, or before her caregiver leaves for the day, gives you the time you need to reconnect with your child, exchange information with her caregiver, gather lunchboxes and bottles, put on coats, and get out the door.

If you need to talk to other parents or to a caregiver, or are preoccupied trying to find a misplaced lunchbox, be sure someone is watching your child. During this afternoon transition, when there are the most adults around, children are often not watched. A caregiver sees that you are there and mentally crosses your child off her list of responsibilities. You assume she is still on duty.

Prepare your child for departure. Just as at the beginning of the day, knowing what to expect at this time will help your child feel more in control, even though she may not be feeling particularly cooperative. Again, give her specific ways to mark the time before leaving, such as "We are going to put your coat on after you jump two more times," or "As soon as you finish your juice, we will be leaving."

Some days you will have to be firmer than others. The combination of being tired, being hungry, and experiencing all the feelings reuniting brings often leads children to fall apart when the time comes to walk out the door. Even though she may protest, your child will appreciate your taking charge of the situation. Your child's relationship with her caregiver deserves acknowledgment that they are parting for the day. Help your child say good-bye and be sure you say good-bye, too.

Settling back into home is your final transition. Karen believes this is the hardest transition of the day:

Changing the guard is tough. When we get home, Paul tests every limit for the first hour or two. He is crankier than usual. He does naughty things. I give him juice and he pours it on the floor. He might throw a toy on the floor. He has a tantrum because he has to come inside while I change my work clothes. He wants to watch his Alf tape but when I put it in the machine, he wants to watch E.T. He doesn't know what he wants. It's easier in good weather when I can let him go out in the backyard.

Sarah, mother of two children, puts it this way:

*The worst part of my day is the hour after I get home. I'm still
buzzing from the office and the kids descend on me while I'm
still dressed for work. You know how kids glop all over you. It's
like being a time traveler, moving from one world to the other.
The transition is hell.*

□ *A Time for Rituals*

Rituals can help smooth out those "hellish" transition times. They
provide adults and children with a sense of order and the comfort
that order brings. Their usefulness starts with your preparations to
leave home in the morning and continues throughout the day.

You may already have rituals for getting out the door in the morning. Perhaps you have a special spot near the front door where your
child sits to take off her slippers and put on her shoes or boots. Your
ritual may be patting the dog good-bye and assuring him that you'll
see him when you come back. If you don't have a ritual, consider
developing one. It can be as simple as singing a song as you load
your child and her belongings into the stroller, or having her carry
her lunchbox from the refrigerator to the front door.

Your child and her special caregiver may have developed their
own ritual for greeting each other in the morning. Or you and your
child may go over to the caregiver each morning together and say
hello.

Rituals can play a comforting part when it comes time for you to
leave your child. Some rituals emerge as the result of the physical
layout of your child's program. Your child and your caregiver might
look out the window in the living room and wave good-bye to you.
Your child might feel better about your leaving after she helps you
push open the big door of her child-care center. Your language may
serve as a ritual ("I'll see you after work just like I always do"). Or
you may find that you always give your child three kisses on the nose
or a giant wave.

Aura describes the special ritual that she and her two-year-old son have: "When it comes time for me to go, we play football. I pretend to toss Bobby back and forth with Joan, his special caregiver. On the final pass he ends up in Joan's arms."

Rituals help at the end of the day, too. Jane carries a bag of Cheerios in her pocket, which she hands to her toddler as soon as she crawls into the stroller. Sonia and her daughter Connie take a few minutes every afternoon to read a book before tackling the job of gathering Connie's things and getting her coat on.

Though your home is a familiar place, a ritual can ease your return and the transition of being back together, even if your child has spent the day there. Susan always has a snack with her two daughters when she walks in the door. For Tom, changing from his business suit to blue jeans indicates to his daughter Wendy that he is now home and available to her.

Chapter 9

Making Connections Between Home and Child Care

You can help your child integrate her home and her child-care experiences, establishing connections that allow her to bring a little bit of home to child care and take a bit of child care back home in the evening. Some connections she will create on her own. These may be as common as her raggedy, but special, blanket, or they may be as unique as a bunch of dried-up daffodils. You and her caregiver can build connections for her as well. Regardless of who makes the connections, they all help your child feel more at ease as she shifts between home and child care.

Children-Made Connections

□ *Objects of Their Affection*

Many children have a special "something" that goes with them everywhere. It may be the shredded remains of a blanket, a rag doll, a stuffed animal such as "Ralph," a dog whose floppy ears Ralph's owner loved to chew, or "Fish," whose tail was furless from all the loving rubbing it received. Tattered, torn, slobbered on, and balding as these objects may be, they are more than meets the adult eye. To their owners, these objects, "loveys" or "transitional objects," as they are sometimes called, are children's way of having their mother with them when they are separated.

Your child may carry her "lovey" everywhere. Or she may ask for it at times she feels under some stress, for example, when you take her somewhere new, if she doesn't feel well, or when she has fallen and scratched her knee. She probably will want her special "something" at moments of separation—when you say good-bye at child care or when you say good night.

Sometimes caregivers do not allow children to bring these special objects to the child-care center. They may be worried that a well-loved object will be lost; also, these rules may be intended to make the caregivers' job simpler by preventing the inevitable "No! Mine!" conflicts that arise when a child rightly refuses to share her lovey. Some programs bring up health concerns: since loveys are often sucked and drooled upon they do have germs. But the assistance they provide a child outweighs any of these concerns.

Besides, keeping up with these special objects doesn't have to be a big chore. Finding one place to keep all the loveys when they are temporarily abandoned can help caregivers keep track of them during the day. A reminder tied to the handle of a child's stroller—"Don't forget Ralph"—can assure that in the rush to get home at the end of the day you don't forget your child's treasured companion and prevent an evening trip back to the center—if it's even open.

When it comes to sharing these very personal objects, you and your child's caregiver can decide what is best. There are some things that are too important for a child to be expected to share. Rather than encouraging your child to share her special object, you can support her by explaining to an interested friend that her dog is important to her and is something she doesn't have to share. But if they are shared and you or your caregiver are concerned about the children's health, remember that children suck on and drool on almost *everything*.

Sometimes adults feel they must "help" a child grow up by taking away her "babyish" object. But this is faulty thinking. Her special object is a tool a child uses because she needs it to cope and grow up. She will let go of it when she's ready.

She'll be ready when she is able to carry inside herself the feelings of *being with you*. Internalizing this connection frees her from having to carry a Ralph everywhere. As this happens, the blankets and dolls will find themselves spending more time in her cubby at child care, until eventually they are abandoned.

Using these transitional objects should help, not hinder, a child moving into child care. If, however, after several months, holding on to an object is preventing your child from enjoying activities (it's difficult to fingerpaint or build with blocks or put together a puzzle if you're holding on to something), it's time to ask how safe and comfortable your child feels in that particular child-care environment. It's time for you and your caregiver to work together to help your child feel more confident and secure.

☐ *Less Obvious Connections*

Children are great improvisers and they are often able to build connections whenever and wherever they need them. It can take some careful looking to recognize the less obvious ones. But if you can recognize them, you and the caregiver will be able to respond to your child more appropriately. Let's take a look at some not-so-obvious connections that children have made.

When Sally, a caregiver, held infant Renee, Renee pinched the skin on Sally's neck. One day, after many "Don't do that's" and brushing Renee's fingers away, Sally noticed that when Renee's mother held her, Renee rubbed her long blond hair between her fingers. Renee's pinching was a connection-making action. But because Sally had short hair, Renee's rubbing pinched and scratched Sally's neck. Instead of breaking Renee's connection, Sally asked Renee's mother to cut her toddler's nails so her pinching would be softened and Sally wouldn't get scratched.

Alex, Caroline, and Laura, two-and-a-half-year-olds who spent the day together in a child-care center, carefully put on their "meeting necklaces" and sat on a large wooden climbing box dangling their feet, not saying a word, having what they called "a meeting." Having a meeting, something they heard their parents talk about often, was a way of having their parents close to them.

As an infant, Leslie spent many hours in her mother's painting studio sleeping in her stroller. As Leslie got older, her mother would offer her the cardboard tubes her paints came in. A month after Leslie began child care, she came carrying a cardboard tube. She held it for an entire morning. It was her connection.

A father tells how his son, Reggie, used his stroller to create a connection:

"The first day at his child-care center, Reggie wouldn't budge from his stroller. He even ate his snack sitting in that thing. When I saw other parents parking their children's strollers in the hall, I tried to pick him up so I could put the stroller away. He began kicking and screaming. I wanted to hide. On his third day of child care, Reggie sat in his stroller for about an hour watching what was going on. Then he climbed out and sat with me on the couch. When a caregiver started to push the stroller into the hall, he cried. The message was clear: His stroller was very important to him. The caregivers kept his stroller in the room for many weeks."

Here a caregiver tells about her favorite child-made connections:

One spring morning, Joany (aged 20 months) and her mother brought in a bunch of daffodils. We found a jar and filled it with water. Everyone came over to see what the excitement was. I told the story of how Joany and her mother had picked daffodils and brought them for us to enjoy. All the children took turns sniffing the flowers. Then we put the jar of brilliant yellow daffodils on the counter.

A few weeks later, while cleaning off the counter, I picked up the jar of now-dried flowers to take to the garbage. Joany

*beamed when she saw the flowers. "Joany ... flower ... Mom-
my," she said. I realized that for her, the daffodils were a connection with home. The vase of dried, brown petals stayed on
top of the bookshelf until the end of the year.*

*During a walk to Riverside Park, Richie picked up a large branch
that had fallen from a tree. As I began my customary speech
about leaving sticks on the ground because they might poke
someone, Richie explained that the stick was his cello. He ran his
hand across the branch singing "de—dah," tapping his toes and
moving his head to the beat.*

*"OK," I said, "we'll take the cello back with us." Richie's dad,
a musician, had recently moved out of the house. I figured
music was a connection with his father.*

*When we got back to the center, Richie, sitting on a milk crate
and using a wooden spoon for a bow, gave us a concert with his
cello. It was the beginning of a ritual. Every afternoon after nap
children would help get the cello out from under the red sofa
and we would have a concert as Richie created a connection
with his father.*

Connections Parents and Caregivers Can Make

Besides recognizing and supporting the connections that children
make for themselves, you and your child's caregiver need to make
connections for your child, too. And like the ones children make,
these can be as mundane as singing a song from child care with your
child at home, or as unique as writing a book with her.

They may also be spontaneous. A mother we know decided to
make noodles for her child's supper. As she drained the noodles, she
realized there was no margarine to put on them. She remembered
that his caregiver sometimes served him noodles and cottage cheese
for lunch and decided to do the same. And as Ben ate his noodles, he
and his mother talked about his caregiver.

You may also have to go a little out of your way to make some connections. A father we know noticed his son Andy waving his hands in the air as he sang in the car one day. The next morning Andy's dad asked the caregiver about this behavior. She explained they had sung "The Eensy Weensy Spider" the previous day. Andy's dad didn't know the song and asked for a quick lesson. That afternoon as his father began singing the song, Andy smiled and joined in.

Parents can leave something special with their child during the day. A handkerchief, a scarf, or even a piece of paper from your pocket with a love note on it gives your child a reminder of you to hold on to physically during the day.

Caregivers can allow children to take something from their child-care program home with them. Although your child might want to take home her caregiver's cat, a better candidate would be something small, durable, and replaceable if it happens to get lost.

Photographs make very strong connections for your child. Unlike children, adults can keep images of absent loved ones in their heads. But we still enjoy photographs and use them to make connections for ourselves all the time. We display them on our bedroom dresser, on our walls. We tuck them in our wallets and suitcases. Photographs give us a very concrete way of having someone with us. They are excellent connections we can provide our children at little expense, and they have a terrific feature: They are easily transported from home to child care and back again.

Photos can help your child "refuel."

Gerry seemed a little mopey. He took a picture of his family out of the basket and rubbed his fingers along it. "Mommy," he said to himself. He put the picture in his pocket and went over to the block corner where he made a line of blocks.

Photos can help your child recall child care when she is home.

Cathy has been at home sick for two days. She sees a picture of Louisa, her special caregiver, hanging on the refrigerator door.

"Wisa," she says, pointing out the picture to her mother. "Yes ...
there's Louisa."

"My dance Wisa," adds Cathy.

"I know. You and Louisa have lots of fun dancing. Tomorrow when
you go back to child care, you and Louisa can dance."

At home or in child care, pictures can be hung at a child's-eye level
on the wall or on the refrigerator, or placed in an album or a "photo
basket." They can be covered with clear contact paper to protect
them from chewing and crumpling. However these pictures are displayed, your child can have with her wherever she goes her mother
and father, her brothers and sisters, her dog, goldfish, caregiver, and
friends.

If pictures are not displayed in your child's center, you may still
give your child the support they offer by taping family pictures in her
lunchbox, or keeping pictures in the pocket of her stroller bag. You
could also offer to make a photo center. Displaying pictures may be
something caregivers haven't thought of or haven't had time to organize.

Books are very special because they allow a child the safety and
security of snuggling up to the person reading with her, while helping her to make connections through the pictures and events in the
story. There are many books on the market written about infants' and
toddlers' lives at home and in child care. Look for books with clear,
easily identifiable pictures and simple text.

But also consider writing books with your child. These books can
be about anything your child knows well: greeting her caregiver at
the door in the morning, things she likes to do in child care, going
home at the end of the day. The text should be very simple and clear.
Illustrations can be simple line drawings, pictures cut out of maga-
zines, or photographs. Don't let the idea of "writing a book" intim-
idate you. The book is really about your child, which is much more
important than how well you draw or whether you have chosen just
the right words.

Here are some sample books:

Mrs. Evans Is Here

BZZZ rings the doorbell.
"Who do you think it is?"
Sheila and her mommy open the door.
"Hello," says Mrs. Evans. "I've come to play with Sheila today."

Laura's Day

Laura is busy.
She feeds the fish.
She slides down the slide.
And eats a crunchy apple for lunch.

Chapter | 10 |

Observation as a Tool

During the time that you and your caregiver are with your child, you may spend hours simply watching what she is doing. But sometimes that watching becomes more than just seeing. You start to observe with a purpose, and this is when observation becomes important as a tool for you and your caregiver to make the most of. Because you and your caregiver make countless decisions about caring for your child based on your individual and shared observations, the better your observation skills the better your decisions will be and the better care your child will receive.

As you observe your child, try to understand from the inside out what she is experiencing. Your child cries. Is she hungry? Wet and uncomfortable? Or does she want your company? Skillful observing allows parents and caregivers to see clearly how a child's unique personality traits, emotions, and developmental stage, in conjunction with her different settings of home and child care, affect her behavior. Using all this information, you can base your response to your child's behavior on the *reasons* behind it rather than just on the behavior itself.

But parents and caregivers don't always observe, or use their observations, as well as they could. Parents and caregivers don't realize that observing can simply serve as a guide to when to intervene. They don't understand that it's necessary to observe a child's behavior from *her* perspective in order to really understand it. And they are not fully aware of how factors they themselves bring to the scene may influence their observations. The purpose of this chapter is to enable you and your caregiver to become better observers and to use your observations to your child's advantage.

When to Intervene

Good observation helps you decide whether you should respond at all to your child's behavior or store the information and take no action. You can decide if your child needs you to step in immediately, or if she requires space and time to work something out on her own.

Often, adults believe that to help a child grow, it's always necessary to interact with her. It's not so. There are times when your child needs you to step in quickly and to take action when her safety is at stake. When you see an infant beginning to chew on a lamp cord or a toddler swinging a stick among his peers during a walk to the park, it's time for immediate intervention. Usually, though, there is time for you to think about your participation. Observing what your child is saying, the way she is holding her body, and the expression on her face can help you decide whether to get involved or to stay out of things and let her manage on her own. While you are watching your child climb between the sofa and chair and then under the table, you may observe that her facial expression reflects keen interest and involvement as she explores spaces of different shape and size. *You're* not so sure she can handle what she's doing, but she gives no indication of any problem. However, when her shirt gets caught on something and she can no longer move freely, you might see her look of involvement change to one of concern or fear. It's obvious she no longer feels so confident on her own and needs some help.

Only by stepping back at times can you give your child the satisfaction of solving a problem on her own, such as freeing a toy that has gotten stuck under a chair, or allowing her the sense of accomplishment that comes with mastering a skill such as pouring her own juice or freeing her snagged shirt. If the toddler's face in the situation above hadn't reflected any change, she probably would have found a way of getting herself untangled and there would have been no reason to help her.

A caregiver explains her decision to simply observe a child playing with a new toy she had made instead of jumping in and showing him how to play with it:

> *I once made a drop-the-clothespins-in-the-can game for children in my child-care program. I set it out on the shelf and observed as Mark began rolling the can across the room. He shook the can, his eyes bright with excitement and pleasure at the rattling sound he produced. It was all I could do not to say, "Wait a minute, Mark. I'll show you. The idea is to drop the clothespins here through this hole in the lid." But I refrained because he was very engaged in the way he was playing with this toy. Two months later, Mark dropped his first clothespin into the can. He sat there for an incredibly long time—almost an hour— dropping clothespins in, dumping them out, and dropping them in again.*
>
> *If I had shown Mark my way of playing the game on the first day he might have done it—or he might have crawled away. One thing for sure is that my intervention would have diminished the pleasure and sense of achievement—and perhaps the frustration—that the rattling can and the disappearing and reappearing pins gave him. I would have been taking away an experience of discovery that is part of growing up. The can and game would have been mine—something I was sharing with him—rather than something that was his.*

Enhancing Your Interventions

The way to enhance your observing skills most effectively is to observe from your child's point of view. It's the best way to see the effect of her emotions and her developmental stages on her behavior.

Observing from a child's point of view allows you to see that a toddler who hits her new sibling is acting out of anger and jealousy. Her hitting is not an uncharacteristic act of aggression, but a reasonable response from a child who's afraid of being replaced. If you respond to her behavior *only,* to the hitting, you might find yourself yelling at her to stop or sending her to her room. But if you can tune in to what she is experiencing, you might talk to her about what she is feeling, or spend extra time with her alone. Observing her behavior from her point of view enables you to address her emotions as well as her outward behavior.

When your child reaches the age when "No" becomes her favorite word, observing will allow you to respond helpfully to some of those negative answers instead of being drawn into a contest of wills. You will be able to see that this is a trying time for her, too, but it's a normal, necessary, and even positive stage in her development in which she is defining herself.

When she says "No" to you or her caregiver, even when you are offering her exactly what she has asked for, be it a cookie or a trip outside, observing can help you feel empathy for her struggle. You will be able to see that although at times it feels as if she is out to defy you, she really isn't. You're able to see that her "No" means "this is me," which is much more important than any issue she might be protesting.

With this point of view, your response to her "No" can shore up your child's sense of self. You can offer choices when she is in the mood to handle them and firm limits when things begin getting out of control.

Observing a temper tantrum from your child's point of view can help you see how your child's feelings build their own momentum. The kicking and screaming indicate that things have gotten out of control, from your point of view, but might mean that they have gotten out of control for your child, too. A tantrum often fuels itself to the point that the issue is forgotten and what's left is simply your child's being overwhelmed by the power of her feelings.

Without careful observation, you might just get frightened or angry at her behavior, and your main goal would be to stop her temper tantrum. But observing from her point of view might encourage you to sit nearby in order to give her a sense of your presence, or to take her in your arms to give her a sense of boundaries. By observing from her point of view, your response can be an attempt to help her regain some of the control she has momentarily lost.

If you observe your infant or toddler from her point of view at mealtime, you'll see that her inability to sit still and her "playing" with her food is a stage in her development. Toddlers spend most of their time actively exploring and investigating their surroundings. Squashing peas and dumping milk on the floor is part of that exploring. The point is, toddlers aren't being bad. They are being themselves.

However, if you look from an adult's point of view you might see it as unacceptable eating behavior, which you have to do something about. To accomplish your goal, you might resort to discipline. But if observing shows that toddlers are just being themselves, why should they be punished? Rather than focusing on what to do if your child doesn't behave the way you want at mealtime or any other time, you and her caregiver can focus on how you can best teach her how you want her to behave. This opens up many different ways of responding. For example, you may try shortening the time you ask your child to sit still, or offering her food such as string beans and slices of turkey that she can easily manage on her own without too much mess. You can continue observing and see what works. It's a positive change for all of you.

When an infant stands on her feet and becomes a toddler, everything in her world changes. Observing the face of a new walker reveals tremendous joy as her world opens up to her. The sense of freedom and the excitement of such new horizons as the top of the coffee table and the third bookshelf off the floor energize her. You will observe that even when she stumbles and falls she gets back up and keeps going. The drive to be upright and mobile is very strong.

Observing can help you understand why a new walker often has so much trouble falling asleep. From an adult's point of view, you would think that, with an increased expenditure of energy by your child, her need for sleep would increase also. You may worry that your child is having a problem. But by putting yourself in her position of suddenly entering a fascinating new world, you can see why it is so difficult to be placed in a restricting crib, let alone be separated from what is going on by closing her eyes and falling asleep. Instead of worrying about her, you can help her by maintaining her daily routines and keeping in mind that sleep will come easier as she adjusts to the new stage in her growth.

Getting dressed is a different experience for your child depending on her age. As an infant, getting dressed is largely a sensory experience and the opportunity to be with you. By the time she reaches toddlerhood, she is a more active participant, sometimes helpful, sometimes not. But along with her ability to help comes the need for her to have more control. So some days she will feel proud about using her new skills and will help put on her own socks. When she isn't feeling cooperative she may strongly protest your or her caregiver's appeals to "get dressed now." Because she cannot yet completely dress herself, chances are you will finally take charge of manipulating her limbs for her, and this goes against what being a toddler is all about.

By understanding your child's strong need for control, you can devise ways to help her have as much control as possible and make the routine of getting dressed easier for both of you. You can give her a warning beforehand that she needs to stop playing and get dressed, offer her the choice of putting on pants or shirt first, and when possible allow enough time for her to participate as fully as she is able.

How You Influence What You See

One last point about observing is that you have to keep in mind that your observations and responses will always be influenced by what *you* bring to the situation—the day you've had, how you feel, and of course your role in your child's life. The following example is a very common scene. Let's look at it and consider what different observers see and how they respond.

Tommy and Luther are playing on the floor in the living room. Tommy is dumping blocks out of a coffee can covered with checked contact paper. He chuckles as four of the blocks bounce off the rug onto the floor. As he crawls over to reach one of them, Luther toddles over and picks up the coffee can. Tommy sees him and reaches for it, screeching "Mine!"

Luther's mother, Tommy's mother, and the caregiver, because of their personal biases, would observe this scene differently and therefore want to respond differently. Luther's mother was brought up in a family that insisted on always sharing. When she sees Luther grab a toy, she hears her parents' words, "You have to learn to share with each other," escaping her lips. She is worried because lately Luther has been saying "no" to getting dressed and to having his diaper changed, confirming her worst fears that she is raising a bully. What will her folks think at Thanksgiving when they see her kid grabbing toys away from his younger cousins?

Tommy's mother will have her own responses. She may encourage him to share or be glad he stands up for what is his.

For Mrs. Hopkins, the child-care provider, this confrontation is a familiar scene. She knows it is difficult for toddlers to share. Today she responds by giving the two a second can of blocks she has made for just such occasions.

How would you respond in this situation? Would you encourage Tommy to share the can? Or explain that since he had put it down, it is Luther's turn? Maybe you would tell Luther that Tommy is playing with the can and blocks and he'll have to wait his turn. If you have a headache you may do whatever is necessary to get the boys to be quiet. You may feel Tommy is selfish for not letting Luther play with the can or that Luther is bad for grabbing someone else's toys. How you respond will depend on who you are and what you observe.

Observing shouldn't be a burden. No one wants to—or can—have their eyes glued to their child all the time. But when you do have a question, remember that observing is a tool you can use to find an answer.

Chapter 11

Resolving Differences

You and your child's caregiver will disagree many times as you share the care of your child. Compromises you made when choosing a child-care arrangement, confusion about who is who in your child's life, feelings about sharing care, lack of respect for each other, not enough communication, being late, lack of time—they all provide fertile ground for disagreement. And, of course, your child's puzzling and frustrating behavior can spark disagreements. Many of your disagreements will simply be a reflection of your personal differences. There are always two sides to everything. But it may still be easy to blame each other when things aren't going well.

Your disagreements will not be harmful to your child, in and of themselves. She doesn't need you and her caregiver to have a friction-free relationship. But she doesn't need to be caught in the *middle* of your conflicts either. Instead of signaling that either you or your caregiver is not doing a good job, or that war has been declared between the two parties, these disagreements should be seen as signs that you and the caregiver need to work even more closely together. When you do disagree, your work involves not only finding a resolution to the conflict but also resolving it in order to prevent a disruption in the supportive relationship you have established for your child.

All the work you have done in building your relationship has laid

the groundwork for dealing with conflicts. You have an understanding of your different roles and responsibilities, and, most important,
you understand how your child benefits when you and the caregiver
work together to support her.

Basically, when you and your caregiver are in conflict, you have
three options. You can resolve an issue without actually confronting
each other, you can work together to resolve a conflict, or you can
sever your relationship. Each can be an appropriate response, depending on the circumstances. Which option you choose will depend on your personal style of handling conflicts and the conflict
itself, its size and relative importance to those involved.

We are going to take a look at conflicts that parents and caregivers
have shared with us. Some have definite resolutions, others do not.
Some are more successfully resolved than others. See for yourself
how these parents and caregivers were or were not able to resolve
their differences. Remember, there are few absolutes. What works
for one child and her parents and caregivers may not be the solution
in another situation. A particular conflict may not even be a problem
for you. It's a personal call. Even if you disagree with how a conflict
is handled, taking an inside look at other people's conflicts may give
you some new insight into your own situation and prove to be
helpful.

Option One: Not Making an Issue of Something

There are many reasons why people decide not to make an issue of
a situation they don't like, or about which they disagree. Some people simply try to avoid conflicts. Sometimes an issue just isn't that
important; no one has enough emotional investment in it. You and
your caregiver feel annoyed for a while and that's the extent of it.
And, many times, a resolution turns up before the problem gets to
the child-care arena.

Not making an issue of a disagreement has different consequences
depending on what the issue is and what the ramifications are for
your child and her child-care experience. In the following stories

you will see clearly how the decision to let an issue ride is appropriate at some times, inappropriate at others.

☐ *Finding Resolutions for Yourself*

In some instances, the possibility of confrontation diminishes when an issue is seen in perspective of your child's total care. Whatever annoys you about your caregiver doesn't stack up against the warm and loving relationship she and your child have built together. And, if you and the caregiver have a strong relationship, there will be plenty of room for tolerating each other's differences. Without this tolerance, many of your disagreements could mushroom into situations disruptive to your child's care.

In the following stories, there exists the possibility of open conflict between parents and caregivers. Different eating practices, different ways of interacting with children, and different values set the stage for possible confrontation. However, when these parents and caregivers weighed the relative importance of the issue that was arising against the needs and best interest of the child, they were able to resolve the problem for themselves.

The Emersons wished that Donna, who cares for their infant daughter and toddler son in their house each day, would not feed their children so many crackers. They preferred their kids to eat more "real food." Donna herself is a snacker. She naturally hands the children a cracker when she has one for herself, and there are times when she knows having a cracker will distract and keep them busy. This isn't the way the Emersons would choose to do it. But when they took a good look at all the good things that happened between Donna and their kids, "We decided that the same part of her that offers the crackers is the part of her that has a lap big enough for both of them." They filled the cracker jar with salt-free crackers and let it go at that.

When Richard complained to his wife that their daughter's family child-care home was not clean enough, she reminded him that they both say the same thing about their own home, where there is only one child, not four. She suggested that a caregiver who is too concerned about neatness might not have the spontaneity of their daughter's caregiver. Talking with his wife helped this father put things in perspective. He took a few days to look carefully at just how unclean the child-care setting was. He saw dust, some clutter of newspapers and toys, some broken toys, crumbs on the kitchen floor, and a bathroom in need of a fresh coat of paint. He also saw the caregiver and his daughter dancing together in the living room. She certainly seemed happy at child care. He took a good look around his family's house where he also saw dust, clutter, some broken toys, crumbs on the kitchen floor, and a bathroom in need of painting. He decided that his daughter's relationship with her caregiver was more important than dustballs. For him the issue was resolved.

A caregiver worked with a child whose parents were, from her point of view, overpowering and intrusive. If Lucy drew a picture and said it was a person, her mom or dad might reply, "No. That doesn't look like a person." They would then hold her hand and guide her crayon as they drew a person with her. Or when leaving, they might say, if Lucy cried, "Don't be a baby. Mommy and Daddy have to go to work."

Instead of allowing these differences to come between them, the caregiver was able to have a broader perspective about the situation. She had the following to say about Lucy and her parents: "Well, I would do these things differently. But remember, this child is in this family for the rest of her life. Her parents are the way they are because of their pasts. She is a strong child who relates well. In their own way, her family gives her a lot of confidence. They let her know 'You *can* do it.'"

A father was confused when his daughter, Lynn, saw a bug in the backyard one day and said "danger." He thought that was peculiar because neither his wife nor he had ever said that to her. They discovered shortly thereafter that the caregiver had been telling Lynn that bugs were dangerous. He and his wife wanted their daughter to enjoy the outdoors and at the same time didn't want to make a big deal of the caregiver's calling a bug dangerous. She was from a desert country and may have been told about dangerous bugs when she was a little girl. The parents decided to handle the situation by saying "no danger" when they went out in the yard with Lynn. In part of the decision-making process, Lynn's parents considered that since she saw them responding differently to the same thing all the time, she wouldn't get confused. Children can deal with adults' differences about bugs. As long as the adults' basic values and what they want for a child are similar, their differences can be interesting and open the world to children. Over time, Lynn will eventually come to her own decision about bugs.

It was the day before Peter's third birthday. He, Ruth, his at-home caregiver, and his mother were discussing his party. "I'm going to have pink balloons," Peter said to Ruth. "No," she said. "Pink balloons are for girls." Peter looked at his mom, who said, "You can have pink balloons and blue balloons and green and yellow and red ones, too." Ruth feels it's not really right for boys to have pink balloons. Rather than getting into a discussion about sexism, Peter's mother decided to deal with the issue indirectly. She wasn't about to try to change what she saw as Ruth's sexist views. They're different people, each with a kind of tolerance for the other. Here she addressed Peter's immediate concern, his desire to have pink balloons at his party, and left it at that.

A caregiver found herself slightly annoyed with a child's parents. The child had a bad diaper rash and her parents continued to forget to supply lotion. The caregiver, looking from the parents' point of view, was able to see that these parents were under so much pressure it was amazing they got their child to child care at all, let alone remembering a new tube of lotion. She took matters into her own hands. She arranged to take all the children on a walk to the corner store to buy lotion. She saw this as a way of getting rid of the diaper rash and providing support for both the child and her family.

☐ *Avoiding Confrontation*

Sometimes parents and caregivers don't make an issue of something because they're afraid to upset the apple cart. Parents are afraid that if they question something—naptime, the lunch menu, or daily activities, for example—a caregiver will quit or take out her frustration on their child. Knowing how difficult it is to find a workable childcare arrangement makes parents hesitate at the thought of having to search for another.

Caregivers, especially private caregivers, can be afraid of being fired if they question or disagree with their employer. And some people will avoid conflict at any cost. If you are not confronting an issue because you don't like conflicts or are afraid of the consequences, it's time to reconsider how you handle conflicts. It's time to trust that the relationship you and your caregiver have developed will carry you through your disagreements.

Not facing a conflict can also leave something "brewing" between you and the caregiver. The issue is there and will underlie all of your work together. Resentment will build, and who knows how it will manifest itself in the end. Disagreements that are left to smolder can only get in the way of caring for your child. The stories that follow clearly demonstrate the problems created by not addressing an issue.

When Nancy dropped her eight-month-old daughter off at family child care, she noticed on a low toy shelf a basket of small beads her child could easily swallow. She put them up on a higher shelf, out of reach. The next day they were on the low shelf again. Nancy wasn't sure what to do. She needed child care desperately, and had searched a long time before finding this arrangement. The care provider was the best she had seen. She was concerned that if she said something the provider would see her as a troublemaker and might take it out on her child or ask her to leave. She ended up moving the basket of beads whenever it made its way to a low shelf and keeping her fingers crossed. The beads were always on her mind.

Her child's safety is really at stake and her child depends on her to keep her safe. There is no way of knowing what would have occurred had Nancy voiced her concern to the caregiver, but the consequences would have been far less harmful to her child than swallowing the beads would have been.

Another caregiver was faced with caring for a child with a diaper rash whose parents also didn't supply lotion. She asked the parents to bring lotion four days in a row, but they continued to forget. She became annoyed because the parents seemed to be ignoring her request, and because they seemed to have such an uncaring attitude toward their child. She also resented that their forgetfulness put her in the position of dealing with a screaming child every time he needed a new diaper. She began avoiding these parents whenever she saw them, which made the situation more impossible to resolve.

When Nicky walked into the center coughing, with his nose running, his caregivers gave each other the "here we go again" look. It had happened before that his mother had brought him when he was sick, and, in their opinion, should have been kept at home. They'd never said anything directly to the mother, but there was definitely tension in the air, quickly resurrected from their past experiences.

The caregivers had their hands full caring for the eleven *healthy* infants and toddlers. When Nicky came to child care sick, they didn't have enough time to give him the extra attention he needed. Their frustration turned into resentment toward his mother. But the mother's job granted her only ten "sick days" a year. She had already used six of them in order to stay home with Nicky, and it was only April. These absences from work were frowned upon. If she didn't take Nicky to child care, she had to pay someone to come to her home— another expense—so sometimes she ended up sending him to child care and keeping her fingers crossed that he would make it through the day. She tried to save her sick days for when he was really sick.

This conflict between parent and caregivers had really developed in part because of factors beyond anyone's control. The mother's inflexible workplace, a budget that didn't allow her to miss a day's pay, a child-care program that had overenrolled in order to cover the rent and other expenses: all these factors added stress to the sharing of this child's care.

Unlike some other brewing conflicts, this problem may not have had an immediate resolution, even if it had been addressed. However, just getting the conflict out in the open and acknowledging each other's points of view can allow the underlying tension to subside and the relationship between parent and caregiver to hold firm. Acknowledging these factors can help parents and caregivers know where to direct their frustrations and energies and remind them they are on the same side.

The parents in a child-care center loved getting notes about their child's day. In the middle of the year, the caregivers were too busy to write personal notes. They just wrote lists of what the children had done. Several parents, in a show of disappointment, would read the lists and then throw them away, right in the child-care center. The caregivers felt angry that their efforts were not appreciated. No one said anything to anyone about it. The bad feelings remained.

Granted, this was not such a big deal. The parents and caregivers still talked to one another about what the children were doing. But even little conflicts left unresolved have a habit of reappearing, most of the time when you least expect it. In this case, acknowledging how important the notes were to parents and how busy the caregivers were could have cleared the air. And, if these notes were not just something the parents had become accustomed to but were really an important part of the "bridge" for the children, the parents and caregivers probably could have worked something out.

□   □   □

The caregivers at a child-care center worked extra hours to plan meetings in which parents would have time to talk together about topics of interest, such as how their children spent the day, setting limits, and sibling rivalry. One mother thought the meetings were a good idea, but no baby-sitting was provided and children were not supposed to come. It was too much of a hassle for her to take her daughter home and then drive back, let alone to find a sitter. Her absence didn't mean she didn't care about her daughter or about the program. She just couldn't manage the logistics. She thought it was more important for her to spend the evening at home with her child. But she did feel put out at not feeling supported for these meetings. Since caregivers weren't supporting her in this instance, how much confidence could she have that they would support her in the future?

The caregivers felt put out, too. They felt their work and contribution was not appreciated. Some caregivers thought she was a bad parent because she never came to a meeting. She was also labeled a bad participant in the child-care program. In other words, even though there was no outright conflict, this parent and her child's caregivers had taken battle positions.

Dwight's family child-care provider agreed to baby-sit one night. She fed him dinner with her family, and then they went out on the porch to count lightning bugs and wait for his parents, who were supposed to arrive by nine. They didn't show up until ten, and then they were annoyed that their son was still up. The caregiver was angry because there was no apology for being late, and no thank-you.

Yet she didn't say anything, perhaps because she was afraid of upsetting the apple cart, or because she was just too tired. And why couldn't Dwight's parents give the respect and courtesy of a thank-you and say "We're sorry to be late"? Maybe they were inconsiderate or saw a caregiver as more of a servant than a colleague. Maybe they were sorry about being late but sensed the caregiver's tension, leading them to take the offensive. Whatever the reason, some tension was left in the air.

Option Two: Working Things Out

When you and your caregiver *do* decide to confront an area of disagreement, you will find that there is no *one* way to settle it. The same conflict may be resolved differently by different parents and caregivers. There is no rating scale you can use to tell how much work or time it will take to resolve an issue. Some disagreements can be resolved easily and immediately, while others take more effort and time. Some disagreements can be resolved by one party taking action or making a change, others need a compromise, and some necessitate repeated meetings over a period of time.

The conflicts between parents and caregivers that are presented below demonstrate the remarkable variety of disagreements that parents and caregivers have, and the unique ways they find to work together in resolving them. They've been divided into two categories: conflicts that were quick and easy to resolve and conflicts that were a little more complicated and took more time and effort.

□ *Quick and Easy Resolutions*   .

Many conflicts are so easy to resolve that they hardly seem like conflicts in the first place. Yet some of the issues involved in the following stories had the potential to cause a major rift. The skills the parents and caregivers have learned in their work together carry them through their disagreements and conflicts rather painlessly and keep the bridge intact.

When the mother of a toddler in a parent cooperative expressed her concern that children might bump into the fish tank and asked if she could move it, she was told by the caregiver that the tank was near an electrical outlet and couldn't be moved because they didn't have an extension cord. "So I went out and bought an extension cord. The next day we moved the aquarium."

The parents at a family child-care program complained to Vicky, the caregiver, about the added sugar in the peanut butter she was serving. She had never thought about it. She had always served processed peanut butter to her own kids and they grew up fine. Vicky felt that the parents were being a little picky, but that looking into a different kind of peanut butter was no big deal if it was important to them. She conducted a taste test, found that the children would eat a natural peanut butter, and bought a five-pound jar made with only ground nuts. That took care of that.

In this example, a resolution was reached quickly and quite easily when a caregiver made a simple change in response to what parents said to her. The parents were pleased about the improved nutrition for their children, and also that their request had been heard and responded to. The sense of satisfaction that comes from working together like this will serve these parents and this caregiver well when an issue that is not so clear-cut, not so easy to deal with, emerges.

Harriet thought her baby son Michael should stay inside on cold days. His family child-care provider felt that going outside was healthy as long as children were bundled up, so she took children outside even on the coldest days. After talking about their differences, Harriet and Mrs. Greene, the provider, decided that Michael could go outside as long as he had on a hat and socks and was under blankets in his stroller.

Hilda, a single parent, was upset that her daughter's center didn't have a man on the staff. She had hoped that child care would be a place her daughter could spend time with a man. She felt that by having only female staff members, the program wasn't meeting one of her child's basic needs. She decided to speak to the center director. When they talked, she learned that though the director had been hoping to have a man on staff, no men had applied for a job that year. So rather than take out her frustrations on the director or the caregivers who were working with her child, she turned to other resources in her life. She talked the problem over with her brother, who volunteered to spend more time with his niece on the weekends.

□   □   □

A mother who was worried that caregivers in her infant son's child-care program didn't always scrub bottles before refilling them took a simple action that took care of her worry. She brought in a large box of bottle liners that could be changed easily each time a bottle was filled.

A caregiver received a phone call one day from a parent who asked how her son was doing. "Fine," said the caregiver. The mother said, "The reason I'm asking is that Brian said you said he drives you crazy. I was afraid you were really getting stressed out." She was also concerned that the caregiver might be taking it out on her son.

The caregiver knew that she had made that statement to Brian. She felt terrible. She didn't want to upset this parent. She remembered that she had told Brian he was jeopardizing her sanity when he kept pulling away from her to try to walk across a path of blocks and go rowing in the wooden boat while she was trying to put his socks on. Out of exasperation she had put her hands on her head and said, "Brian . . . you're driving me crazy."

Over the phone she assured Brian's mother she hadn't been angry, just exasperated. His mom said that was what she had thought.

There is no way this mother could have known what was going on without asking the caregiver. And many caregivers might not have been comfortable enough to be so open about what they said. Care-givers are only human. It can be difficult for them to tell parents who want things to be just right that they've had a hard day or ran short of patience or lost their temper. You can imagine where this conflict might have gone if it had been left to brew.

The Conners asked Mrs. Dawson, their caregiver, to be sure to take young David out for a walk around the neighborhood each day. That was fine with her, but it became a hassle when one of the wheels on the stroller got bent. She wasn't going to mention it for fear they would think she had broken the stroller, but then decided to take the chance. David's father said that he had hit a rock over the weekend while taking David for a walk and had forgotten about it. In five minutes he straightened the wheel.

A bent stroller wheel may not seem like much, but when it comes to a caregiver worrying about her job and you worrying about the care of your child it is easy for each of you to lose perspective. Confronting the issue directly let Mrs. Dawson see there really wasn't a problem. If she had been too afraid of possible repercussions and not spoken, she would have been worried about nothing. In this situation, talking resulted in simple, direct action and set the stage for continuing the policy of talking and working together.

A father tells about his daughter who just turned three: "For a few weeks Becky had been having temper tantrums. We met with her teachers to talk about what to do. The teachers wanted us to use the reward system—rewarding her when she was good. Well, that didn't sound right to us. I wanted her to learn to behave. I didn't want to bribe her to be good. We told the teachers we didn't want to use the reward system and they said OK. As it turned out, the tantrums stopped in a few days anyway."

In this situation, parents and caregivers met and talked. They clearly had different ideas of what to do and shared these ideas. The caregivers were able to let go of their ideas and follow the parents' approach. Becky may have been moving through a new stage, or her parents' and caregivers' new approach to her behavior may have led to the end of her tantrums. We can't know for sure. But we do know that there was a united front to help Becky through her tantrums.

Roger was frightened and angry the day he arrived home early and couldn't find his two children and their caregiver. Fifteen minutes later, they walked in the door. The caregiver explained that she had taken the children to her daughter's house, just a few blocks away, for the afternoon. She thought the visit would be a nice change for the kids and for her. Roger said she was welcome to take the kids there, or other places around town, for that matter, as long as he knew where they were. They made a plan. Each morning, the care-

giver would tell Roger if she was planning a trip. If by chance something came up unexpectedly, she would leave a note on the kitchen
table under the fruit bowl. The caregiver and Roger's children spent
lots of nice afternoons at her daughter's home and other places in
the neighborhood. Roger felt that he always knew where they were.

Something else worth noting happened here. Until the day the
caregiver took the children out of the house this father and caregiver
hadn't realized they needed a policy about such trips. They were
learning together as they went along.

The caregivers at a child-care program used paper towels to clean
children's bottoms when they changed diapers. The parents of one
infant decided to bring in a giant box of diaper wipes for their child.
They labeled the wipes with their child's name and asked the caregivers to please use them. They were upset to find the wipes nearly
gone after just one week. As it turned out, caregivers and parents
were using them for other children as well. It was pretty clear that
wipes were preferred over paper towels. Because they weren't in the
program's budget, the choice was for everyone to bring their own
wipes or to contribute to a "wipes fund" and buy a case of them for
the center. The volume purchase was voted the most convenient and
least expensive way to go. Now there are wipes available for everyone. Bringing in wipes began a gentle wave of change that could
have turned into a storm over an empty wipes box if parents and
caregivers in this situation hadn't been able to communicate and
work together to make a plan. All the children ended up being a little
more comfortable and their parents and caregivers felt good that
there were wipes available for everyone's use.

A father talks about how his son's caregiver handles situations differently than he does: "I think Pam lets Kenny get away with too
much. At home I'm more strict than she is. I want him to share his
toys when he has friends over. I want him to clean up his toys. When
she and I talk about it she tells me that it's hard for kids his age to
share, and that it's asking too much of him to pick up his toys. She

does seem to know what she's doing. The way I figure, at her house she's the boss and we'll do things her way."

□ *Turning Up the Heat*

The following conflicts involve much stronger emotional investment on the part of those involved than those that were quick and easy to resolve. These conflicts usually have more than one issue behind them, are more complicated, and take more time and more effort to resolve. If you find yourself in a similar situation, know that continuing to work together will help you find a solution that satisfies you and the caregiver and continues to support your child.

Sarah, a caregiver, tells of being so angry with parents who were habitually late at the end of the day that she couldn't look at them for months. "Speaking to a colleague helped me see that there were two issues. One, the matter of these parents' being fifteen minutes late every day. Two, the matter of why it was so difficult for me to express my anger. I realized the fifteen minutes was a rather simple issue compared to my feelings. Well, I had a meeting with the parents. I reminded them of the closing time. They apologized and made it a point to be on time. And since then, I've been learning a lot about myself and anger. I've realized that in my family we used to tiptoe around anger. Being angry isn't such a terrible thing. Knowing that means I don't have to wait for months to deal with a problem—weeks, maybe, but not months!"

Shirley was furious. Her son Rob had diarrhea and she was sure it was because he was in child care. She made an appointment to speak with Denise, Rob's special caregiver. Denise didn't look forward to the meeting. It seemed that something was always upsetting this mother. Rob had had diarrhea before and it turned out he had eaten too much applesauce—at home. And yet, diarrhea is a major health concern in child care. Denise couldn't just brush it off.

They met. By pooling their ideas, they developed this strategy: (a) The program's health committee would be notified and asked to review sanitary procedures such as washing hands and cleaning the changing table; (b) Rob would eat only the food his parents sent for a week; and (c) Denise would clean out the refrigerator, being sure to remove leftover food.

As Shirley and Denise talked, Shirley's fury died down. She felt listened to and able to share the underlying feelings that had made a case of diarrhea, which did need to be addressed, feel like a crisis. She told Denise that when she came to pick Rob up in the afternoon he had been busy and shown little interest in her. "I'm afraid I'm missing his life," she continued. "I have to tell you that when I saw him drinking from a cup at child care, I almost broke into tears. He's grown up so fast."

Denise was taken back. She suddenly saw Shirley, who she had always seen as a fussy, rather demanding parent, in a different way. Shirley's openness helped Denise feel some compassion for her and understand that they were partners. Denise was able to listen and be there for Shirley more than she had been. She shared with Shirley her picture of the different roles they played in Rob's life. Shirley felt this responsiveness. They ended their conversation with both a plan to deal with the immediate problem of diarrhea and a better understanding of each other.

One afternoon Charles came to pick up his daughter Anne and found her hat was missing. He and his wife work very hard to assure Anne's well-being, right down to the details of carefully choosing her clothes. It was upsetting that the hat had been lost. He grilled each caregiver about when they had last seen it and made sure they knew he *expected* them to find it.

The caregivers knew Anne's parents had waited a long time to have her, and they wanted to support them as much as they could. They had always tried to be very careful with Anne's things. They, too, were concerned when the hat turned up missing. What might be a small thing for some parents was not for Anne's. However, when Anne's father gave them "orders" to find the hat, they felt he had really overstepped his bounds. They also felt he didn't have any

understanding of the special care they did give his daughter's possessions.

One caregiver, Mary, spent two days looking everywhere for the
missing hat. She put up a sign, walked back to the park where Anne
had spent the afternoon playing, looked through the cubbies, and
sorted through the lost-and-found box. Nothing. The next day she
was helping Anne put on her coat and pulled the hat out of the
sleeve. When Charles came in that afternoon, he said, "Great, you
found the hat." Mary laughed. "Charles, it was in her sleeve. Don't tell
me you've put her coat on for two days and didn't see it." He shook
his head and laughed with embarrassment and some relief. "I guess
I owe you thanks and an apology."

Jim turned pale the day he walked into a child-care center classroom
and found his two-year-old son, Louis, wearing a barrette. "Hey,
Louis!" he said as he went over to pat his son on the head. "What are
you doing with this silly thing in your hair?" He removed the barrette
from his son's hair. "Let's get your things together so we can go
home. Maybe we'll have time to play baseball before dinner." The
caregiver noticed that Jim seemed a little flustered, but he left so
quickly she didn't have a chance to speak with him.

The next morning she raised the issue. She explained that right
before he came, many of the children, both boys and girls, had
wanted to try on a barrette because Andrea, a new student teacher,
had barrettes in her hair. Trying on a barrette was one of their ways
of getting to know Andrea. Jim admitted he had been very upset. He
had been raised to believe that barrettes are for girls. He said his wife
accuses him of being a sexist, and maybe he is. He wants Louis to
grow up to be a man who can take care of himself. But Jim was
willing to consider that wearing a barrette was a way of getting to
know someone, even as negative feelings from his childhood were
evoked. "I just know my father would have been furious if he had
been here."

Over the year, Jim and Louis's caregiver sometimes talked about
the "barrette incident." He later said it led him to do a lot of think-

ing about how he was raised and what it meant to be the father of a boy.

Grace's daughter Lynn came to child care wearing a pretty new dress. Grace was upset to return at the end of the day to find that Lynn's dress had a streak of blue paint on it. The dress had cost a lot of money. She was proud to have her child wear such a nice outfit and angry that the caregiver hadn't been more careful, but she was uncomfortable about saying anything directly. So when she was putting Lynn's coat on she said loudly enough for Terry, the caregiver, to hear, "We'll have to tell Terry to be more careful about not getting paint on your dress."

Terry heard but didn't say anything. Parents talking to her through their kids had always annoyed her. It had been a hard day working with substitutes—two regular staff members were out with the flu. Terry felt she couldn't give anything else to anybody.

After a good night's sleep and the return of one of her coworkers, Terry addressed the issue of the paint on the dress directly with Lynn's mother the following morning. She apologized. Then she explained that like all two-year-olds, Lynn moves fast and had painted not only on the easel, but on her dress before Terry could stop her. Grace, in a hurry to get to work and still a bit annoyed, couldn't stop and talk.

Two days later, after Grace had time to think about things, she was better able to put her daughter's needs in the forefront. She and Terry talked about how much Lynn liked to paint, and because painting meant getting some on her clothes, it would be better for her to wear old clothes to child care, or at least bring in an old set of clothes that she could change into for painting and other messy activities. They agreed Lynn would wear old clothes to child care and on the special days when she was dressed up, would change to painting clothes.

Caregivers were upset because Cheryl arrived late every morning. Though the program was flexible enough to avoid unnecessary pressure on parents in the morning, caregivers encouraged parents to arrive by 10:00. They saw Cheryl's arrival at 11:30 as disruptive, because they had to stop to help a child get settled in for the day when everyone else was well into the morning. But the late arrival was particularly bad for Cheryl because she would arrive right as everyone was beginning to clean up for lunch.

Cheryl's mother, Peg, enjoyed the time she spent with her daughter in the morning. Also, it was hard for her to get Cheryl out of the house. Part of the reason was that Cheryl was two and wanted to do things her way and only when she wanted to do them. Part of the reason was also probably that Peg had some ambivalent feelings about bringing Cheryl to child care.

The head caregiver in the room felt a bit torn. She knew it was important for Cheryl to have time with her mother in the morning. She also knew the way things were going didn't work for Cheryl in terms of the child-care schedule. So she decided to talk with Cheryl's mom about what was happening. Cheryl's mother said she would try to get Cheryl there earlier.

Nothing happened for a few days after the conversation. The caregiver wondered if she should say anything else. She felt a little frustrated that Cheryl continued to walk in the door at 11:30. And then one morning Peg happened to observe Cheryl begin to build a zoo with blocks, one of her favorite activities, but before she was finished, she had to put them away for lunchtime. Peg saw that this was frustrating and confusing for her daughter. Seeing the situation through her daughter's eyes helped Peg see that her current schedule wasn't working for Cheryl and caused her to decide to make a change.

Glen was biting. His behavior had a direct impact on children in the center. Some children had been hurt, and others who had escaped the teeth marks sensed something in the air. Glen himself was frightened and at times out of control. He didn't plan to hurt anyone. Biting is a scary thing to do. Something needed to be done.

But the tension at the center made it difficult for the adults to talk together. Glen's parents were angry at him, embarrassed that their child was biting, and concerned about why he was doing this and how they could help him. They would come in and get out of the room as fast as possible. Parents of the other children were worried their child would be bitten next, and perhaps worried that their child would begin biting, too.

The caregivers were not immune to the tension. They worried that these biting episodes made it appear that they were not doing a good job. Previous experience with biting kept them from panicking as they tried to figure out the best way to help Glen. His parents and special caregiver arranged a conference. Talking together, they found they had more helpful information than they were aware of. The caregivers knew that some toddlers bite for a certain time and then no more. They had also noticed that Glen was more likely to bite at times when things got confusing or he was crowded in a small space, such as the cardboard-box house. His mother had noticed that Glen bit when he became agitated at home trying to keep up with his older brother and his friends.

Together his parents and caregivers decided to guard Glen from overwhelming situations, such as wrestling matches with five-year-olds at home and crowded boxes in child care. Glen's special caregiver took responsibility for keeping her eye on him and tried to be there when he needed her to help him stop biting. The other parents relaxed a bit, seeing that something was being done. Maybe because his adults were doing something, maybe because he felt their support rather than their anger, or maybe because he had just needed a little time to settle into a new stage of development, within two weeks Glen was no longer biting.

The mother of a toddler didn't want her son to take a nap in child care so he would fall asleep early at night and she would have time to finish the work she brought home from the office, do some laundry, and maybe even have a few minutes to relax. The caregivers felt that if he fell asleep he needed to sleep. The caregivers realized they had something invested in this decision, too. Naptime is traditionally the only time of day when caregivers can take a break, have some time to talk with one another, and eat lunch undisturbed. They look forward to children's naptime.

His mom and caregiver talked together. They tried to balance the mother's needs for some time in the evening with the child's needs for rest during the day. They decided that if the toddler fell asleep, the caregivers would wake him up after an hour. Neither party was completely satisfied with the plan. But it seemed to work for the toddler.

Parents at a child-care co-op were dismayed at the physical plant. The floors were never cleaned, the tables and chairs were sticky, and sheets in the nap room were turning gray. After speaking among themselves, they arranged a meeting with the caregivers who were responsible. During the meeting, it turned out that the caregivers were also unhappy with the way the room looked. Working in such a grubby setting made it hard to feel good about themselves as professionals.

There was a discussion about who was responsible for maintenance and cleaning. Parents thought it was the caregivers but the caregivers disagreed. Although they would do daily cleaning chores, they weren't hired to scrub floors. At the salary they were being paid they didn't feel they should have to be housekeepers as well as caregivers. Parents considered the option of hiring someone to clean the floors but decided it would be too expensive.

A plan was agreed upon that called for rotating groups of parents and caregivers to meet once a month on a Saturday morning to scrub the floor. Caregivers said they would be more careful about keeping the chairs and tables clean. Parents agreed to be responsible for taking their children's sheets home once a week, washing them, and bringing them back. They decided to evaluate how things were going in three months' time. After the first month, things reportedly were going well.

Discussing the issue revealed that what appeared at first to be an issue for parents was an issue for caregivers as well. No one would have known this if parents had kept their complaints to themselves. Instead, the situation would have been ripe for strong undercurrents of "us" versus "them." Airing the issue gave everyone a chance to put their feelings on the table and develop a plan agreeable to everyone that involved everyone's making a change. Setting a date to evaluate how things were going kept the door open to discussing this issue again and revising the plan if necessary. In the meantime, everyone had a sense that something was being done.

Imagine this scene.

"Hi. I began toilet training Lenny [two years of age] over the weekend. I brought these in case he has an accident."

Fran, Lenny's mom, hands Alice, a family child-care provider, a stack of five pairs of underpants and pants.

That afternoon Alice hands Fran a large plastic garbage bag filled with wet clothes.

How would you feel if you came to pick up your child at child care and found him wearing diapers the first day you sent him to child care wearing underpants? How would you feel about spending a large part of your day wiping up puddles from your living room rug and having to change a child six times? How do you think it would feel to find yourself soaking wet and have someone interrupt your jumping on pillows and building with blocks six times in order to change all your clothes?

There are several possibilities of what has gone wrong and it is up to the adults to figure out the best way of handling the situation.

Perhaps Lenny did use the toilet successfully at home over the weekend and today had a bad day, or simply found it to be too much to keep up a new skill at child care where there were other people and activities to distract him from remembering to use the toilet. Maybe at home he depended on his mother's constant reminders, which his caregiver was too busy to reinforce.

Perhaps Lenny's mother was ready for Lenny to be toilet trained before he was. Toilet training has certain prerequisites: the cognitive ability to recognize signals, the physical maturity to control muscles, and on the emotional side, self-control. It's very common for parents and caregivers, in their eagerness to be through with wet, smelly diapers and struggles with changing uncooperative two-year-olds, to decide the time for toilet training has come before a child is ready.

The task of the adults is to figure what is happening. To do this, they need to talk together. Alice needs to know exactly what Fran means when she says she began toilet training. Was Lenny able to say he needed to go to the potty, a sign that all systems are go? Or did Lenny spend the weekend sitting on the toilet at regular intervals, so that he happened to be there when he had to urinate or defecate—a sign that Fran, not Lenny, is ready for toilet training?

Fran and Alice may each need a little more information about toilet training to decide if Lenny is indeed ready to wear underpants. They may find some books and articles helpful, or talking with a pediatrician or the mother of a recently toilet trained child.

Taking everything into account, the adults will come up with a plan. Perhaps they might decide to give Lenny another day wearing underpants, or perhaps what they find out about toilet training will lead them to wait for Lenny to tell them he's ready. Another day of puddles that ends with a mountain of wet clothes is a vote for waiting.

The Colemans felt that Beth, the caregiver who cared for their daughter, Noreen, gave her too many sweets to eat during the day. They suggested that rather than stop at the bakery each day, Beth could stop at the fruit market and buy herself and Noreen a piece of fruit instead of pastry. They asked her to please stop bringing sweets for Noreen. If she wanted to eat some, she should do so when Noreen was sleeping. Beth agreed. Four days later, they discovered a bag from the bakery in the garbage can and, when doing the laundry, they found chocolate on one of Noreen's dresses. When they asked the caregiver about their findings, she said she bought a doughnut one day and wouldn't buy any more when she was caring for Noreen. She seemed very uncomfortable and didn't say more than that.

Here the tension centers on more than nutrition. Noreen is clearly in good health. There are two issues that bother her parents about this situation. First, they are concerned that the caregiver is not respecting their parental authority. As we have emphasized through-out this book, parents must be the boss where their children are concerned. This caregiver is clearly not doing what they ask. Second, they want to be sure the caregiver doesn't just say "yes" to them and then go ahead and do whatever she wants. Their concern is that if the caregiver is not honest about what she feeds Noreen, she may not be honest about other, more important things.

The Colemans don't want to fire Beth. They've felt until now that she does a good job. Noreen seems to like her. And looking for a new caregiver would take more time than they have. They've tried to figure out what is happening from Beth's perspective. Did she forget their request? Did she want to avoid a scene with Noreen when they walked past the shop and Noreen insisted on a doughnut? Does she need a doughnut to begin her day? Does she like the coffee and people in the shop? Is she feeling possessive—feeling that she should call the shots when she is on duty? Is she purposely disobeying them?

Noreen's parents again requested that Beth not give Noreen sweets. Again they tried to make a plan with Beth that met her needs, suggesting that she buy a doughnut on her way to their house in the morning and eat it when Noreen was napping. Beth responded by saying OK. They decided to give the situation some time to see what happened.

A child-care provider wanted the parents she works for to put their child, Fran, to sleep before midnight. They kept her up in order to have time to spend together in the evenings. As a result, Fran was a real grouch when the caregiver arrived at eight, and she ended up sleeping much of the afternoon. Her caregiver believed that Fran was missing too much of the day.

Fran's parents agreed with their caregiver when they understood how their child's late bedtime was affecting her. They talked together several times and devised a few different plans to revise Fran's sleeping schedule. They tried not giving Fran a nap in the afternoon with the hope she would fall asleep earlier in the evening. She fell asleep at dinner, only to wake up a few hours later. They tried letting her sleep only two hours during the day, though the caregiver felt bad about waking her up. For now, Fran's parents are stepping back. They think focusing on the situation has added perhaps even more pressure to bedtime. Though Fran's sleeping schedule is still not the best, there is no underlying tension between her parents and her caregiver now and there is still collaboration. The bridge here is strong.

A mother asked a caregiver what was going on. Her daughter Donna had been coming home saying that another child had been hitting her. The caregiver began to get tense because the fact was that another child *had* hit Donna, but she had not told Donna's mother. Afraid that her employee would think she was keeping things from her, the caregiver began talking about how two-and-a-half-year-olds are learning to play with one another and sometimes resort to hitting.

The mother said she wasn't worried about Donna's being hit. She knew that some hitting was part of learning to play with other children. Instead she raised the question of whether Donna had been worried about *her own* hitting. This started the caregiver thinking. It made her recall the day that Donna had pushed another child off the slide and had gotten upset when he cried.

By talking together, this parent and caregiver discovered that Donna was really telling her mother that sometimes she feels out of control, and this is scary. They talked about all the ways they could think of to help her deal with her feelings. They considered reading books with her about feelings, encouraging her to say loudly "I'm angry," and to stomp her feet when she was upset, being there to try to help her stop hitting and to comfort her as well as the subject of her blow. They decided all these ideas sounded helpful. They agreed not to make too big a deal of a common developmental occurrence, but to apply their ideas both at home and in child care. Parent and caregiver left their discussion feeling more in tune with Donna and each other.

Option Three: When Conflict Means Changing
the Roster

This is an option no one likes to think much about. It is certainly not one to take lightly. The core of your child's child-care experience— her relationship with her caregiver—takes time to build and is not easily changeable. Switching child-care arrangements is disruptive. But it happens.

You may feel that you made a mistake in your choice of a caregiver or program. Maybe you did. Rather than seeing a necessary change as negative, consider it a positive statement about your involvement in your child's care. This is not to say you should jump at the first thing that goes wrong. But if, over time, things cannot be resolved in a way you are comfortable with, you need to act.

The need to change can appear after one day in child care, after two weeks, or after two years. The issue that is the catalyst for change will be different for everyone. The bottom line is that when the kind of care your child is receiving is no longer acceptable to you, or caring for your child is no longer tenable for your caregiver, it's time to change. The following examples may be helpful should you find yourself contemplating drastic action.

One parent said, "We decided, based on her references, that one woman was going to be the one. We met her and we hired her. Two weeks later we fired her. She spent all afternoon watching TV."

Another parent reported, "After a week, I realized she was not right. She was overstimulating. She was 'at him' all the time, singing, touching him, demanding his response."

One parent changed caregivers when her infant daughter grew into a toddler: "For a while, I had Laura with two people who were opposite sides of a coin. One was playful, outdoorsy, and more a disciplinarian. The other was very loving.

"Now that Laura is older I want her with someone who does

something. I let Nicole, the loving caregiver, go. She kept giving Laura a bottle and putting diapers on her, even though Laura didn't do any of those things anymore. But now I'm worried that maybe she doesn't get enough hugging."

"Having Jason, our second baby, has changed things. Now Mrs. Arnold has become very attached to him. She tends to leave Andy [three years old] on his own. He pokes at the baby, hits him and occasionally pinches him, which I don't want him to do, but Mrs. Arnold is *too* harsh with him, calling him a 'bad boy' and sending him to his room. She and Andy have been together Monday through Friday since he was five months old and now here is an intruder whom she dotes on.

"We've been agonizing for six months about getting rid of her. You have to take so many factors into consideration. I felt, 'How could I let her go? She is the bedrock of my life . . . the linchpin.' Deep in my heart I feel gratitude and indebtedness. Everything I've been able to do at work, I've been able to do thanks to her. There wasn't a clear-cut reason to make a change, only our feelings. Our family situation and kids outgrew her. There was no longer a good match for us.

"We talked with her. We tried to give her suggestions of what to do. I'd tell her, 'Mrs. Arnold, I don't want you to call Andy a bad boy.' We talked with her four or five times over the year. I don't think the developmental aspects of the situation were available to her. She sees things in terms of behavior: Andy is bad if he hits the baby. She feels we are being too soft with him.

"She was fine when Andy was a baby, but she doesn't have the energy to go to the park, to keep up with two children. She doesn't have the creativity to keep both children happily occupied.

We were planning a move sometime soon, and now we are going to tie it in with changing caregivers. If things with Mrs. Arnold were as good as they had been, we would put up with our small space. Moving will make it easier to make the break with her."

□   □   □

The parents of a five-month-old withdrew their child from a program in which the caregivers fed him on the standard schedule without paying any attention to whether he was hungry. They talked to the caregivers and wrote down their child's particular schedule. They even tried telling the caregivers he had his last bottle at home an hour after he actually had, with the hope they would give him his bottle an hour later when he might be ready for it. Nothing could swerve them from their rigid feeding schedule.

Sometimes it's caregivers who insist on the change. Nora, a family child-care provider, relates how she had to ask a mother to take her son out of her care: "On the contract I give parents a month's trial period. You wouldn't think it would be necessary. I get along with almost everyone, but once there was a baby I just didn't get along with. It's hard for me to admit. I tried for two weeks. He cried all the time. The hardest thing I've ever done is to tell that mother, 'I think it would be best if you tried someone else.' She cried because I wouldn't take care of her baby. Child care is scarce and parents get scared. But as it turned out the mother was glad I was honest. She found another place. And sometimes, almost a year later, I take care of this child when his caregiver is on vacation."

A mother of two daughters begins this story: "By the time she was twenty-eight months old, Debbie was toilet trained. She only wore diapers at night. Well, we sent her to child care in underpants and she had an accident one day during her nap. She is a very sound sleeper. The provider told me to bring diapers and I said OK, but Debbie was to wear them only for naps. That night I put fifteen diapers on the ironing board to take the next day. I figured that would be enough to last a while."

Debbie's father continues: "The next morning we forgot the diapers. When I got to child care, Louise, the care provider, asked 'Where are the diapers?' I said we had forgotten them. We live a half hour away but she said, 'I want the diapers now.'

"You'd think she could have let Debbie use another child's diapers just for once. You might say I 'lost it.' I went to the store, bought diapers, and threw them in the door at her. And then I called my wife at work and said she should begin making calls because we were taking the kids out of there.

"We found out what happened. It turned out Debbie had peed on Louise's brand new comforter. Well, she was taking care of kids. I'd think she would be prepared for things like that happening. And why would she let a kid sleep on a brand-new blanket?

"When I went to pick the girls up Louise asked me for an apology. It was a Wednesday. I paid her through Wednesday and took the girls out.

"We weren't sure about her as a caregiver from the beginning. Looking back . . . but how do you know for sure? I guess you just have to trust your gut. One day when I picked up Debbie her eyes were red. I could tell she had been crying for a long time. I worried that the caregiver was too strict but I didn't say anything. I didn't want to stir up trouble.

"I might have known things weren't right when I'd come in the afternoon and find the caregiver watching *Home Shopper*. The girls would be playing on the floor near her. But then she gave the girls nice birthday parties. And my sister had recommended her. My sister was upset when things didn't work out.

"But how can you know about everything? Louise was certified by the state. You figure that must mean something. Maybe she was just getting burned out. She seemed OK at the beginning. Now we've hooked up with good child care. I would recommend it to anyone. The teachers are easy to talk to. They listen to what we say. There is a whole range of personalities. An older, grandmotherly caregiver makes the kids breakfast in the morning. The younger caregivers like to do active things. It's almost like a family."

Conclusion

Parents and caregivers we interviewed while writing *Sharing the Caring* described themselves as coworkers, conurturers, and cooperators for kids. However you choose to describe the relationship between you and your child's caregiver, your child needs the two of you to work together to build a bridge between her worlds of home and child care.

As you collaborate to help her feel safe, secure, and happy, you each play a unique role in her life. You, her parent, are the most important person in your child's life—her base. Your caregiver can offer a trusting relationship, but no caregiver, regardless of how much training and experience she has, can ever take your place. Your child has the capacity to care for more than one person at a time. The affection she feels for her caregiver doesn't diminish the love she feels for you. Your caregiver isn't your competitor. She is your ally.

Developing a partnership with a caregiver can enrich both your life and that of your child. You will have the comfort of knowing you are not alone in the awesome task of childrearing. There is someone else with whom to share the questions, concerns, and joy—someone who knows about children and who cares about your child. Feeling the support in your relationship can lessen the stress that is part of being a working parent balancing the needs of work and family. You can relax a bit and be more available to your child.

By sharing information and observations with the caregiver, you have a chance to see your child through another pair of eyes. Because she has some distance and objectivity, a caregiver often sees things that a parent's total involvement with her child doesn't allow. Getting another perspective is an opportunity to learn more about the unique individual who is your child.

The safety and security that you provide your child when she is apart from you helps to make her first steps into the outside world successful. The satisfaction and pride that you feel about having supported your child and that she will feel about having "made it" will color the other "firsts" in her life. When the day comes for her to begin school, to have her first overnight at a friend's house or to go to summer camp, you will both have a sense of confidence that comes with your history of good beginnings.

As you stretch and grow in your relationship with your caregiver, you will be learning more about your own feelings and values as well as gaining new communication and problem-solving skills. You and your child can only benefit as you become more aware of yourself as a parent and as you develop skills that you can use in your relationships with your child's doctor, and later, her teachers.

In *Sharing the Caring,* we've offered information and skills for you to use in building a good working relationship with your child's caregiver. Whether you've recognized what you do every day or have discovered new ideas you want to try, take what is relevant to your situation and make it yours. Together, you and your child's caregiver can make child care work for your child.

Index

accidents, handling of, 37
activities:
  "daily activities" curriculum and, 38–40
  in-the-field investigation of, 38–41
age of child, in choice of child-care arrangement, 19
agreements, precaregiving, 29–30, 80
at-home care, 19, 23
  child-caregiver ratio in, 25
  childproofing in, 36
  emergency procedures in, 37
  getting to know place in, 84, 86
  illness policies in, 37
  increasing visibility in, 26
  in-the-field investigation of, 28, 32
  reliability in, 26
  socialization opportunities in, 27
  see also private caregivers
attention, child's need for, 24–25
attitudes, in parent-caregiver relationship, 69–73

bedtime, parent-caregiver conflicts about, 145–46
beginning child care, 83–92
  first days in, 83–84

getting to know one another in, 88–91
getting to know place in, 84–88
reacting to newness in, 91–92
benefits, for caregivers, 29
biting, 140–41
books, 35
  as connections between home and child care, 112
  writing with child, 112–13
budgetary considerations, 21

caregivers:
  checking references of, 28, 32–33
  child-free time needed by, 59
  child's connection with, 48
  child's trust in, 48, 49–50
  expert role assumed by, 62–64
  high turnover rate among, 69
  interviewing of, 28, 29–31
  in-the-field investigation of, 28–33
  isolation or boredom of, 25
  objectivity of, 50–51
  observing of, 28, 31–32
  parent's guilt taken out on, 68
  parent's jealousy of, 64–66
  parent's relationship with, *see* parent-caregiver relationship